When
IS THE RIGHT TIME
TO SELL MY BUSINESS?

The expert answer from
RICHARD MOWREY

FREE! The 35 Questions
Any Serious Buyer Will Ask You...
Find Your Buyer's Question Checklist at:

www.RichMowrey.com/Buyers

Published by: Groundhog New Media

ISBN 978-0-9978801-0-6

Version 2016.8.15

Book Interior and E-book Design by Amit Dey | amitdey2528@gmail.com

Table of Contents

Introduction

We all know how difficult the public and private investment markets are to navigate. The underlying drivers in these markets continue to change over time. Financing for transactions is often constricted. The number of active, strategic buyers varies. Private equity groups change their industry preferences. Consequently, it is difficult, although not impossible, to get optimal pricing and terms for the sale of a privately-held business. The odds shift in your favor if you know when to sell your business and how to get ready for the biggest transaction in your life.

As a professional intermediary, I have been repeatedly asked:

"When should I sell my business?"

When I hear this, I know this is one of two important questions these business owners have been asking themselves. Although every business and every situation is different, I always give these business owners the same answer. This book gives you that precise answer and a lot more. It provides an overview of the tools and techniques that I have used to facilitate the successful sale of numerous businesses over the last three decades. I invite you to benefit by learning from my years of experience as a business valuator and intermediary. The book is designed to clearly show you what to do... and how to do it. This book will also help you focus on the when and the why...as you learn about "the answer" so you will not only know...

The best time to sell your business.

You will also know about the value enhancement and other actions required to get the very best results for you and your family. As you begin this important "knowledge seeking" effort it may help to reflect on a quote by Jim Rohn:

"We must all suffer from
one of two pains:
the pain of discipline
or the pain of regret.
The difference is
discipline weighs ounces
while regret weighs tons."

Chapter 1

The Answer

As noted in the introduction, most business owners ask themselves two questions over and over again. These two questions are:

What is my business worth?
And...
When is the right time to sell my business?

The answer to the second question is simple. But it generates a series of new knowledge acquisition, purposeful action, and timing questions!

The answer is:

When the business is ready!
When you are ready!
And... When the market is ready!

The complexity comes from the interrelated nature of the three-part answer. There are many new questions generated in order to answer the primary questions in detail. The optimal sale will occur if, and only if, you can systematically find the answers to the new array of questions. This first group of new questions are:

When will the business be ready?
When will you be ready?
When will the market is ready?

Along with an understanding of the newly developed question:

How will you know...?

These critical determinations are required to advance the development of an ideal ownership transition event.

From a 10,000-foot view, the business will be ready for sale when all of the significant elements are in place. To achieve an optimal price and terms, you must show qualified buyers clear evidence of the business's valuable attributes.

Historic performance: A business will be ready for sale when historic performance analysis provides proof that existing processes can deliver consistent, positive results. Historic financial statements are the starting point for this analysis. This work is the foundation for value measurement and enhancement. Assessment of other operational factors should be initiated as part of these early steps. Astute buyers will compare the business's operating characteristics to known standards for success. These risk and reward assessments are the basis for preliminary purchase decisions by qualified buyers. Historic performance analysis must show an acceptable balance between risk and reward. This balance is a requirement for a qualified buyer to take the subsequent steps in the purchase process.

Future prospects: Business evaluation analysis starts with historic performance. However, this is simply the beginning for the more important determination of the future prospects for the business. Buyers analyze history for the primary purpose of estimating future performance. You, the business owner, have benefited from past performance of the business. The buyer is seeking to benefit from future performance. Oliver Wendell Holmes Junior once stated:

"All value is based on a prophecy of the future."

It is the prophecy that provides price support to justify commitment of capital by knowledgeable buyers. Economic and industry analysis is a part of a buyer's foundational work in this important area. Financial history and future expectations build the larger story.

Growth plans: An important aspect of the future picture is the growth rate of revenue and cash flow. And the projected consistency of this growth. Although a business with a strong marketing and sales department can effect notable growth in a slow growth industry, it is certainly better to be operating primarily in an industry that has a strong growth pattern. Operation in growing market segments within an industry is a clear plus for valuation.

Consequently, buyers are going to be looking directly at both the company's and the industry's revenue and gross margin trends. Acquirers want to see that the company is growing faster than the underlying industry. Sellers need to recognize that evaluation of growth is a major determinant of the final transaction price. If a business has strong growing customers in industries with equally strong growth, it is significantly easier for a buyer to pay a higher price. Buyers will not only accept but expect internal planning to reflect these growth patterns. Additionally, having newer products in place or in the pipeline to support growth plans will be viewed very favorably by astute buyers.

Management: Past performance is a clear indicator that management has made good marketing and production decisions. Similarly, future growth plans, supported by product development and repeatable sales processes, are clear evidence that management is operating at a high level. All professional buyers will quickly look to see if this past success is driven by a small number of managers or whether there is a cross-functional team in place to support future growth. The value of the business and the ease of transfer will be directly reflected by the quality of the management team in place.

"Look at me, I'm the only one around here that can do all this!"

5

Systems: Goods management develops and utilizes outstanding systems to foster repeatability and continuous improvement. Historic performance provides sound evidence of how these repeatable processes work. Excellent hiring, training, administration, marketing, and sales systems add value to any business. Conversely, to the extent that the business operates without formally or informally documented and repeatable systems, the business will be viewed as less stable and less valuable.

Risk profile: There are lots of things in any business that can introduce and increase risk. Customer concentration, vendor concentration, a limited management team and many other things add risk. Buyers are going to assess the balance between risk and reward. The reward comes from extending past growth and performance patterns. The risks come from consideration of the potential negative changes. Mitigation of the risks will go a long way toward increasing the value and ease of transfer of the business.

From that same 10,000-foot view, look at the type of considerations needed to get ready for the biggest transaction of your life. A lot of this has to do with effective planning. Experts suggest that the average business owner of a midsize growing business should spend 25 to 50% of her or his time in creating plans. Most of the remaining management time should be focused on implementing, measuring and adjusting those plans. Development and execution of value enhancement programs are nearly 100% of the effort required.

Specifically, the following types of plans need to be developed for you to be ready to sell your business:

Personal financial plan: We all know that personal financial planning should be an ongoing process. However, if this has not been the case for you and your family, you're not alone. Only a very small percentage of people take the time to focus and prepare financial plans. This financial backdrop is critical in both personal and business decision making. If you don't have a personal financial plan, now is the time to put one in place! Fill in the blanks of the future so that you know where you want to go and what you want to do. This is a baseline step toward positioning for a transfer of the ownership of your business.

Certainly, knowing the value of your business will be a major factor in your personal financial plan. If a business valuation has not been part of the ongoing measurement and management of your business, now is the time to change that. Preparation of a valuation as an input to financial planning is critically important.

Take this step as soon as possible to fully assess all of the assets you have at your disposal for the future. Certified financial planners and business appraisers are the two professionals that can help you in this area.

A good initial step toward personal financial planning is to list the assets that you have today that contribute cash and to make a separate list of the assets that consume cash. Then determine which of those assets are going to be maintained in place following an ownership transfer of your business. *(Do this for personal edification before engaging a professional financial planner.)* The difference between those two numbers will give an indication of the gap that must be filled by the proceeds from the sale of your business. This analysis helps you set the specific objectives required to start this next phase of your life.

Family plans: You may have already passed over many of these financial hurdles. Your age and the makeup of your individual family have a direct effect in this area. Planning for college tuition, maintenance of real estate, and sporting assets should be highlighted in your personal financial plans. This is a very important part of what you want to do for your family.

Life insurance for you and your spouse will play an important part in this family planning effort. Fully and openly assess the ultimate future you want to create and any contingency plans required. You want to take these variables into account as early as possible. Knowing that you have completed all the steps in this very personal area will give you the comfort to proceed with business and other planning.

Estate plans: It is crucial to understand the impact of both taxation and non-financial elements on the settlement of your estate. Estate planning should provide important feedback to your financial and family plans. It is shocking how many esteemed business women and men die without an estate plan. It is more shocking to see what this lack of coordinated planning can do to families. Ideally, you should be visiting your personal attorney to update your existing will on a regular basis. Estate plans should change as circumstances change. Updates are in order for business owners of every age and every stage of their business and personal lives.

The beauty of plans is that they provide a baseline for adjustment or change over time. As business plans change, the additional information developed should be used in related decision-making. Your personal financial goals and objectives are the drivers of the transaction price required. Having adequate life insurance and sufficient liquid assets minimizes concerns about the estate process. Well-drafted legal documents are critical to the implementation of estate plans. The financial inputs to the estate plans are key considerations in the sale of your business. Painful as this work may be at times, it will give you peace of mind and pay its own type of dividends.

Charitable plans: You, your spouse, and your family may have charitable organizations that you been working with over many years. Many business owners defer charitable involvement due to the time consumed by their business. Charitable plans can be easily implemented as long as they are considered early enough in the planning for the sale of the business. Surfacing desires and playing accordingly is the key. Your financial and estate plans should prompt effective actions to ensure success in this area. Timing of charitable contributions vis á vis your business sale may make a significant difference. Good planning with professional advice will help you make the most effective decisions.

Clearly, the interactive nature of the planning required in these above areas is self-evident. In addition, working to enhance business performance is the driver of all of the projected results. Achievement of price goals in the business sale process provides the antici-pated financial resources. These specific assets are the components of the financial and estate plans. To the extent possible, all of this planning should take place in parallel. At a minimum, outlining of plans in each area will help solidify the relationships between the plans. Those steps are going to be critically important. Adding focus to the underlying decisions and value drivers is a bonus gained from integrated planning.

All of this planning should take place in a very orderly manner. These plans will be influenced by the per-sonal assessments that you have or will make. There are major areas of personal assessment to help crystal-lize your personal readiness to enter into the process to effect the sale of your business.

These measureable areas are:

Interest in the business: You may or may not have started your business. But you probably have managed it for a period of time if you are seeking inspiration to optimize the sale. Assessing your level of interest in developing the business further is an important deter-mination. If you are not challenged and excited daily, it may be time to consider selling your business. Do you get the same joy today when the company secures a new key customer as you did years ago? Do you look forward to training and mentoring members of the management team? Do you delight in seeing both the business and employees succeed? Or, has your enthusiasm in these areas waned or at best gone through periods of high and lows.

It is quite natural for your level of interest and intensity to change over time. Different is OK. Indifferent is NOT. Start by comparing your engagement today to when you were first guiding your business through early stages of growth. It may be clear to you that you do not have that same interest. It is more likely that you find yourself looking elsewhere for challenges. These are clear indications that you are nearly ready for an ownership transfer.

Energy: Do you have the same focus and ability to bring your energy to bear to solve critical problems? Are you still leaning forward to provide the needed momentum and action? Do the daily challenges of the business actually energize you? Or do you feel like they easily diminish your personal drive?

All business owners go through highs and lows. It takes special people to start and manage privately-held businesses. The ability to accept risks and act accordingly is unique. Business ownership requires a certain type of person with an abundance of energy.

Business cycles are found in most every industry and certainly most businesses. These cycles can take a toll on the energy continuously needed to manage the business. Recognizing that there's a difference today from yesterday in this area is a key factor. Changes in this personal attribute suggest a readiness to reduce the daily burden of management.

Other interests: The majority of business owners spend an inordinate amount of their time working on and in their business. A few do this to the total exclusion of other interests. Outside interests such as recreation and community involvement may not exist. Unfortunately, this is not the picture of just a small segment of business owners.

It's important to look at yourself and your family and see what your outside interests are. If your outside activities are broad and you know where you want to spend more time, that's fantastic. If these interests don't exist or haven't been developed there is work to do. Developing the discipline to carve out this time may be harder than you might think. Understanding where you are and what you can and will want to do goes a long way towards effectively moving yourself into the next phase of your life.

Emotional attachment: For many business owners, their business has three types of value. It has an intrinsic value, a market value, and an emotional value. If the emotional value outweighs the other two, it may be very hard to transfer the ownership of your business. This is simply your attachment to the interaction with employees, the customers, and the vendors. There also may be many, many, many great personalities that you've had the benefit of interfacing with for years that you do not want to change.

There is also your perception of yourself with and without the business as seen by your family and the community. As a business owner, you are naturally viewed as a community leader. Once you have sold your business this may or may not change. But it may change in your mind. This is the assessment and hurdle that is important to understand and address before taking any steps to sell your business. If you or members of your family are not fully prepared in this area, there are steps you can take to get ready which will be addressed in later chapters.

The third critical driver toward a positive decision to sell is:

When the market is ready!

Market Readiness: When we talk about the market, we are talking about an economic system with a lot complexity. The market for privately-held businesses has its own set of players with many moving parts. The key to market readiness is an understanding that an individual business owner can control very little. However, a deep understanding of how the market place operates helps with navigation. A business owner can craft strategy development positions to provide for market cycles. By applying knowledge, business owners can benefit from the movements within the marketplace.

In many ways, this is like piloting a small boat on the ocean. The ocean has any number of crosscurrents that can push a boat along or hold it back. Also, small boats on the ocean can encounter quick squalls or major weather events. The experienced captain will navigate at all times with these things in mind. The same is true for the owner of a privately-held business. Specifically, every business owner must contend with the national and international economic activities. A keen awareness of the direct and indirect impact of the larger economy on customer demand is absolutely essential. This knowledge is critical for strategy planning and development. It also helps to determine optimal tactical steps.

The broader economy will affect the business's primary and secondary industries. Most businesses operate directly or indirectly in market segments or within a group of industries. The business must contend with changes in all of these market segments. Understanding the cyclical economic trends is the first step toward determination of market readiness.

In any given marketplace, unless it's highly unique, every business owner contends with a group of competitors. These competitors may be current or prospective companies. Knowledgeable competitors will act to benefit from overall economic activity and specific industry trends. Knowing how your competitors operate, think, and act are key inputs into market timing.

The broader economy is regularly influenced by the actions of the financial community. In addition, any given industry will, at times, be in favor or out of favor with the financial community. These qualitative differences in the financing environment follow observable trends. The quantitative measures of rates and lending limits exhibit similar trends. These trends must be viewed with an eye toward the direction of change as well as the rate of change.

To best prepare for the push and pull of the marketplace, a business owner should set up systems of measurement. Spotting early trends is an important input into business and personal readiness. An outline for the assessment of these systems will be provided in subsequent chapters. Trend analysis will help heightened awareness of the effects the marketplace will have on price and terms.

You now have an overview of the three critical components in the answer. Until the answer is deployed to your benefit, you will probably keep posing the question. It is time to stop silently asking the question and to start formulating the answer. It is time to focus on the answer more often than the question. This will smooth the way ahead as you continue along your business ownership path. *(The graphic provides the building blocks for the answer. Note the business is the foundation.)*

When... all three are READY

You want to begin the process of developing specific tools and techniques. These are the tools and techniques required to assess and assemble the three components of the answer. These tools and techniques will help you determine:

- Where each of the three key components are in development
- Whether they are sufficiently positioned to reach your objectives.
- What to do next
- How to do it
- When to do it
- Why to do it

The assessment methods can ultimately make all the difference in keeping you focused on improving the readiness of your business for an eventual sale. The effort will pay huge benefits as you prepare for the biggest transaction in the life of any business owner.

Chapter 2

Start to Understand the Answer

In this chapter we begin to look at the methods and practices to assess the three components of the answer. This is the process of learning what to do to achieve major progress. Along the way, you will begin to crystallize a picture of the business...When it is ready. When you are ready *and*... When the market is ready. The ultimate aim is to have all three components ready either when the opportunity arises or when you decide to create an opportunity.

Many business owners delay decisions required to help identify what needs to be done. All business owners have the option to assess where they are today regarding the three parts of the answer. Lack of action is essentially an acceptance of things as they are now. You can do that...as many do. Or you can start today preparing for the most potentially rewarding transaction in your life.

There is a simple way to think about what you want. It is as follows: The objective should be to ultimately sell without regrets! To do that you will want to work towards a transaction that is on your timetable, on your terms, and at your price. To succeed you want no second guessing.

Do all of the elements in the business transaction have to be like rifle shots at the center of a long distance target? No. But they should be sufficiently clustered on the center of a reasonable target. Alignment in this manner is what provides assurance that there will be no regrets. When you complete the most important business transaction of your life, you do not want to be second guessing or having anyone else do it for you!

"What do mean it's blank and shows no future for my business? Did you try re-booting?"

Most transactions are unplanned: This is a most unfortunate fact. This is what you are endeavoring to avoid by gaining the knowledge and following the process identified in this book. We will take a look at some of the reasons that prompt business sales. All too often business sales take place in an untimely manner. They occur when neither the business owner nor the business are appropriately prepared.

Customer or vendor change: If the business is dependent on a key customer, the risk perception increases. Any dramatic change in the relationship or in the customer's business can have a significant impact. This can occur in any number of ways. The customer may make strategic decisions which change the relationship or end product requirements. Or, the customer may have found one or more new suppliers at better prices or terms. With good customer communications and a focus on service this should never happen. Unfortunately, at times it does. More importantly, buyers are well aware there is risk of this occurring.

Alternatively, the customer may have been part of a transaction. This could easily be an acquisition where the acquirer has alternate vendors. Differences imposed on purchasing plans may reduce or eliminate sales to the key customer over a relatively short time.

Transactions of this nature could also take place from the other side of the operating equation. A major vendor could be acquired. The acquirer (maybe one of your competitors) could reassign output. Or they could raise prices, or change the level and types of service. Such action could significantly impact the historic business relationship.

Loss of either a key customer or key vendor can often be a transaction catalyst. The changes force action based on the performance results. The business may have made considerable investments in capital equipment to serve the specific needs of the customer. Those investments may become sunk cost in equipment that is not readily adaptable to the other market opportunities. Unused capacity of this nature may cause financing sources to execute on their rights under prior agreements. Such steps to assure repayment are normal and can prompt early consideration of a business sale.

Many businesses build marketing presence and service around a particular vendor. Losing the vendor's brand precipitously may not allow the business time to reposition itself in the marketplace. Long time purchasing relationships may have provided the company with attractive margins which may be lost.

It may not be possible to reestablish similar margins with one or more new vendors. Depending on the operating level, a key vendor change can have a direct effect on cash flow. It also may often have a more important indirect deterioration in employee attitudes. Things like this should not happen that way, but unfortunately they do!

Industry or technology change: Any business operating in a volatile industry sector must weather ups and downs. However, if the industry change is more than just a cyclical event, it may impact the business far into the future. Adaptability is required to survive. If present, this is a wonderful attribute.

Demand can drop quickly due to technological developments. This is the old buggy whip story that we've all heard discussed for decades. This is precisely the reason that business buyers will be looking for companies in industries with a positive outlook. A major plus exists if the company has technology on the leading edge of industry trends. Risk comes from the inability to foresee, plan for, and adapt to industry and technological changes. All too often industry changes prompt inopportune transactions to satisfy financing sources. Recognition that this can happen and how it might happen is the first step toward mitigation!

Owner's personal changes: There may be a few business owners who are not optimists, but very few. Business owners in general require a mindset to look past risk. That is how they can work diligently to develop near-term and long-term rewards. This same mindset often causes a business owner to look past or not prepare for a variety of possible problems. These can be in their own health or family life.

Most, but not all people, are fortunate to have excellent health through the bulk of their working career. Unfortunately, even someone in excellent health can be involved in an automobile, train, plane or other accident. Such events can result in a period of long term recovery or death! When this happens, the sale of the business is almost immediately a subject for discussion, if not action.

Business planners often sensitize business owners by discussing...what they characterize as...the **dismal Ds**. These are disability, divorce, and death. Clearly, any one of these three requires specific planning to assure family and business continuity. Regardless of the planning, the dismal Ds can still drive an unplanned transaction. In such a case, the ultimate business sale is going to be significantly less than optimal in any number of regards.

Unexpected offer: Just like the loss of a key customer or vendor an unexpected acquisition offer can prompt an unplanned transaction. Obviously, this is more positive when something of this nature takes place. However, if the business isn't ready for sale or if the owner isn't ready, the opportunity may be lost or partially squandered. Business owners may be very much aware of how attractive their business is or can be to others. But they are often surprised by the source and timing of unsolicited acquisition offers. Without some preparation and planning in advance of such an unexpected event, the path to closing can be very bumpy at best.

Overstated picture of readiness: Ideally, you want the business to be ready for sale at all times. That's the key to the success that you're looking for. Obviously, you also want to be personally prepared enough to consider an attractive sale option knowing an offer might arrive in an unplanned way.

Many, many transactions ultimately take place is an untimely manner. Given the propensity for such events to occur, it is critically important not to overstate the readiness of your business. You want to be able to make a consistent, clear-headed assessment. The desire to know where you are in this process is important to develop usable knowledge. This requires an understanding in three specific areas:

- First, valuation and value enhancement
- Second, business transaction processes
- And third... What sells... and ... What does not!

Valuation basics: Let's take a look at what drives value. Value measurement can be expressed in a simple equation:

$$\underline{Value = Income\ /\ ((Rate\ of\ Return) - (Growth\ Rate))}$$

Income (measured as net cash flow) in this equation is the reflection of business performance. In other words, this is the reward of ownership. The rate of return required by a prudent investor is the measure of risk. This is the mechanism used by an investor to account for the potential of not realizing the reward. And, the growth rate shown in the equation is the anticipated future linear growth rate of the reward. Obviously, this is the reward growth represented by business performance improvement.

Another way to look at this equation then is: Value is a function of:

- Business Performance *(in other words the REWARD)*
- divided by the Business RISK Measurement
- modified by the GROWTH RATE of Performance *(the REWARD)*

Future benefits create value. The growth of benefits (the reward) increases value. Uncertainty, expressed as the risk of not actually achieving that result, reduces value. Stated another way, the value equation is:

Value = [Business Performance] / [Investor Risk Rate] – [Performance Growth Rate]

As an example, if projected cash flow for a business is $1.5 million and the investors required rate of return is 20% and the growth rate of the projected net cash flow is expected to continue into the future at 5%, the value equation would be as shown below:

Value ($10 Million) = $1.5 Million / (20% - 5%)

For those who have some background in the academic or investment field, this is recognized as the classic

Gordon Growth Model. This rudimentary introduction will be expanded to emphasize the basis for each part of the measures in this equation in order to take a deeper look into valuation and value enhancement.

© Michael H Marks

"Hey Mr. Brokerman, are you sure there wasn't a faster way to get us to the closing table?"

Sale Process: All phases of planning and preparation require understanding of the sale process. Knowing what your business vehicle needs to be outfitted with and how it needs to be maneuvered is a major plus. This is true for three reasons. The marketing and closing of the business sale is a very technical process. It involves more than 200 steps that need to be completed in the right sequence and with the right emphasis. It is also a very emotional process.

Lack of preparation can make the technical part of the process significantly more difficult. And last, the process may take much longer, at times, then originally planned. The planning horizon for most midmarket transactions is 12 to 18 months. This timeline does not include preparation time. The 12-18 month period reference is how closely "closing" follows the first marketing activity. Some businesses will close much earlier. The vast majority will fall into the 12 to 24 month timeframe and a few will take longer. The patience required to maintain business performance can make a dramatic difference. Maintaining business momentum during this technical and emotional process will make a significant difference. You, the business owner, control the type of result achieved.

It's instructive to remember that only one out of three deals close in the middle market in the originally planned manner. These statistics are terrible. You do not need to be concerned about statistics in the end. You want to be solely concerned about completing the transaction on the right terms at the right price. Acknowledging that there will be huge ups and downs helps to keep focused. In the end, this process requires three things: **knowledge, preparation, and persistence!**

What sells: Development and use of knowledge about what sells can be the X factor in a transaction. The marketplace defines what "good" businesses are. Using this information directly in the preparation model increases value. At the top level "what sells best" depends on whether:

- the industry is in favor
- the business has a defensible market position
- the business has excellent growth trends (revenue and cash flow)
- the business has acceptable diversification of products, customers, and vendors
- the business has an effective management team based on proven performance results
- the business has documented systems in place that provide for repeatability of marketing, sales, production, and administrative processes

This list of attributes are all inputs to investors' decisions. These elements cannot be separated from the analysis of historic business performance.

The buyer's projection of future results is in great part based on this information. In addition, they are a major part of the risk assessment that any prudent buyer will apply to their valuation work. All of these elements are also important in transaction structuring. But if a buyer cannot be convinced that a substantial market opportunity exists, the review process is likely to stop there. (i.e. operating in an industry with favorable growth trends is a transaction accelerator.)

Ideally, the industry should be clearly recognized as an investor favorite. It is important to look for and measure growth characteristics. One simple requirement, for most buyers, is that the industry should be growing notably faster than the gross national product (GDP). In addition, it should be evident that new investors are committing new capital.

If the business passes the industry test, then the market position will be diligently assessed. Professional investors are looking for a defensible competitive edge in a particular market segment. They want to see one or more product groups in leadership positions in the market. And, ideally they would like to have new products in development to add to the competitive defensible market position.

Growth trends sell: Let's quantify what sells:

- Revenue growth at or above the industry trend and greater than 8 to 10% on a consistent basis
- Gross margin growth at or above industry trend and improving
- EBITDA > 15% as a percent of sales with absolute growth
- Cash flow growth greater than 8 to 10% with a strong indication that this growth rate can be maintained or improved

Experienced business buyers recognize what can be. But, to act they want to see solid evidence of momentum in revenue growth, margin expansion, and increasing cash flow.

Less is more: Less operating leverage sells. Why does it sell? Buyers are looking for operating models that minimize risk if the revenue growth projections are not achieved. What this means is that businesses with high gross margins are more attractive. Obviously, <u>all businesses keep their financial records in a somewhat different manner.</u> However, in general, gross margins should be above the comparative gross margins of the industry.

Buyers want to find operating models with reduced risk. As a first test they are looking further on down the income statement hoping to see high EBITDA margins. EBITDA margins greater than 15% are often the lower threshold for discipline acquirers. This level of the net profitability affords the buyers an additional safety factor. This reduces the impact of an unexpected cyclical downturn or other revenue contractions.

Experienced analysts will include the annual capital investments (CAP-X) required to maintain capacity, on a cash basis, in lieu of depreciation. This is a key part of the income statement analysis. ... less again is more. The lower the required annual capital investments, on a recurring basis, the better. This is an area that can impact cash flow particularly in constricted earning periods. This is all about risk management for the buyer. *(Note: For this discussion, all of the financial analysis is assumed to be based on "normalized" income statements.)*

Diversification sells: As noted earlier, buyers look carefully at various types of the diversification. This procedure is to determine the proper level for the risk measurement used. Customer diversification is number one. The largest customer should represent less than 15 percent of total sales. The top 8 to 10 customers should normally be less than half of total sales. This target profile reduces the risk associated with the loss of a particular customer. Unfortunately, a customer loss can certainly happen through normal market actions. And occasionally as a result of the transaction itself.

© Michael H. Marks

"Quit feeding him so many bananas! He's our biggest customer, what if he falls?"

Vendor diversification can be equally important when it comes to risk assessment. Buyers do not want a single supplier to be critical to the offerings the company is making in the marketplace. Risk is reduced and value is added if there is solid evidence you have a viable secondary supplier. You want to have backup suppliers in any area that might affect product quality or service.

Finally, although it is not always possible, multiple product lines should be contributing to sales. Such varied product sales should be clearly measurable. Additionally, different products should add notable gross margins to the planned future performance.

The proprietary nature or patent-protected products is an additional plus. Such formal protection is not essential but it is helpful. These assessments are part of the continued risk measurement by the buyer. Perfection is not required. Often positive movement in a meaningful direction may be enough to mitigate excessive concerns. However, a knowledgeable business owner should be aware that <u>different buyers may have dramatically different views on product diversification</u>.

Target financial profile: A buyer's picture of a desirable business is definitely going to vary by industry. It's also going to vary by buyer or buyer groups. What private equity groups may be looking for can be significantly different from what strategic buyers may be looking for. The required profile may also vary radically depending on what else the buyer owns. In some cases, the financial profile may be less important than the product line or the customer base to be transferred.

Private equity groups (PEGs) are significant buyers of midsize businesses today. With that stated, it is important to have some understanding of what they are seeking. These buyers generally break down target acquisition into to two groups: Platforms and Add-ons.

Platforms are PEGs' initial investment into an industry or industry segment. Platform companies are typically businesses with sales greater than $15 or $20 million (ideally $ 25 million and up). Occasionally, private equity groups will make lower initial investments in a specialty industry sector. Such investment as low as $10 million are the exception.

Add-on investments are made once the PEG has an initial position in industry. Add-ons can be of any size in theory. Transaction values for add-ons are most often going to be greater than $5 million. There are exceptions here if the target can quickly add revenue growth or if there is a unique factor present.

The related metric with a private investment group is the target EBITDA measure. The vast majority of PEGs are looking for initial investments in businesses with this earning measure greater than $4 million. And most PEGs will only consider add-ons with EBITDA greater than $1 million. These metrics are the result of the time and costs involved to complete an acquisition of any size.

This does not mean that you have to have this financial profile in place today. These are simply metrics to consider in planning and developing work. The idea is to put your business in the path of the buying groups with the most investing prowess and capital. Good growth planning and achievement moves a business's sales and earnings quicker than you might think. Compounding is one of the wonders of the world and is a true wealth driver for business owners.

Strategic buyers, unlike financial buyers, may be significantly more interested in non-financial assets. They may be specifically seeking other attributes of the business. Technology processes, products, open production capacity, market positions, and technical management leadership may all be drivers for specific acquirers.

A deeper dive into these areas is called for. When you begin strategic planning efforts pay particular attention to the SWOT analysis. What is important to note at this point is that strategic buyers are less driven by financial metrics than by other assets. That does not mean that they will not use poor financial performance results as a tool against you in price negotiations.

Proven management skills sell: Have you ever had a friend, who owns a business tell you how great his marketing and sales staff are? And then you later learn that revenue in that business has not grown for over three years. You might ask then, if they are so good why have they not produced sales results?

There is nothing better than established performance trends to confirm management abilities. These results directly assess existing management... either positively or negatively. Proven management skills sell. Skill levels should be evident via the performance measurements throughout the organization.

If the past financial trends are clearly positive, buyers will want to know why. What they're looking for is diversification of positive contributions. They want to see that there is no single individual or manager who are solely responsible for the positive results. In the ideal situation, sales should be driven by multiple managers and staff members. There should be strong leadership in each functional area. These managers should each be capable of promotion in the future. In simplest terms, the business should have three or more experienced managers in place. Preferably this team has been in place for a minimum of 3 to 5 years. This is the type of management experience and diversification that will add to salability.

Proven systems and processes sell: Historic revenue and cash flow trends provide solid confirmation that:

- repeatable marketing and sales systems are in place

- effective quality control systems are in place
- production and delivery systems are in place
- strong administrative and financial controls are in place

Historic financial statements should confirm that existing processes are delivering above average performance. And comparative reporting should show margins and growth exceeding the industry metrics.

Where you are: Truly understanding "where you are" regarding your financial, personal, and family plans is important. This is certainly not the area where you want to kid yourself. Almost every professional business advisor has seen the negative impacts from delayed planning. There is a big downside in those situations where people think they have plans in place that turn out to be insufficient. The lack of an effective buy/sell agreement can have an incredibly negative impact on your business and family. Similarly, inadequate estate planning can exacerbate an already difficult situation.

You really want to assess your financial position and how you ultimately will get where you want to be in the future. This must include the interactive planning required as well as personal assessments. You want to measure any changes in your energy level, personal interest, and emotional connections with the business. These are not areas where things that can be deferred.

Understanding the market impact: As a beginning point, you want to look at global, national, and regional economic cycles. Then determine the position of your businesses therein. Just developing methods to collect information can be very helpful. Data assembly should focus on your industry and competing industries.

A detailed look at financial markets can be helpful. Assessing alternative investments as well as interest rates can be equally instructive. Chapter 7 will address these issues in detail. Finally, a sober assessment of what capital is available today is essential. Once understood, an analysis of future capital sources will help develop a foundation for success.

Market assessments and timing are all about balancing risk and reward. There is certainly a risk of holding a business too long. Or, there is a risk of acting too soon. We can all look back over the first decade of this century and see what happened in that regard! It's all about being prepared... to make a judicious decision. Part of good preparation is testing "what if plans" on a regular basis. This is all part of the work necessary to **complete the biggest sale in your business life at the right time!**

Chapter 3

Getting the Business Ready

(Value Assessment)

Preparing the business for sale is an ongoing process. It is clearly where you should initially focus the vast majority of your efforts. If you need a reason beyond having your business properly prepared for sale, it can certainly be the myriad of ancillary benefits. These benefits will accrue on a daily, weekly, monthly basis as you improve the performance of your business. Clearly there is every reason not to delay. Immediate action is required!

Should you start by painting the building, hiring a new salesperson, or calling your best customer? Should you get busy on the new product you want to develop? No... You may do all these things eventually and many more. To line up the "preparation improvement steps" correctly, you want to start with a thorough evaluation of your business.

> Disraeli said it best:
> "Action cannot guarantee
> to bring you happiness;
> but there can certainly be
> no happiness
> without action!"

This preparation phase is all about knowledge acquisition. First you want to learn where you are with your business and then determine where you want it to go. To prepare your business and have it ready for that optimal future transaction, there are a combination of things you will want to do.

You want to develop a picture of the business "when it is done". If you can't crystallize this picture today, that's fine. That simply means you need to acquire more knowledge to work up a vivid result. To help paint the picture, you want to carefully diagnose the situation as it is today.

This second part of the readiness program following the diagnosis is planning for action. The third part of this process is to take these planned steps in the right sequence. This is the effort that will permit you to move the business toward increasing readiness for sale even though there may be more to do. And finally, throughout this process, you want to minimize the potential impact from the dismal Ds... disability, divorce, and death. (Business health is important. But your personal health is more important!)

One of the incremental steps is to develop an understanding of what is to be sold. If you look at your balance sheet, assuming it's like many privately held businesses, you will find assets that are not part of the operating business. These are assets that can either be retained or liquidated separately. Mentally separating these assets on the balance sheet will help you to begin to develop the first limited picture of your future sale.

What we are talking about is not the Penn State season tickets. Although season tickets of this nature can all too often become a debatable part of the transaction at a later date. What we are discussing is the things that fit the owner's particular interests. These assets may or may not be integrated into the method of business operation. These are assets such as a private plane that would not normally be part of the future transaction. In addition, marketable securities or owner's life insurance policies clearly qualify as separable assets. These and any other non-operating assets can and should be retained.

In addition, the real estate owned and used in the business should be reviewed. This real estate may be owned by the operating entity or by the shareholders. Most professional business acquirers prefer to allocate cash for use in operational growth. This desire supersedes most investments in real estate. Consequently, unless it is special-use real estate, you should begin thinking about who should ultimately own the real estate. And, if retained, under what terms and conditions you would structure a lease.

As you review your balance sheet, it is important to remember that all assets are stated in accordance with accounting standards. What this means is that all assets are shown at book value. Book values shown on your balance sheet may have little to do with an actual market value. Consequently, additional analysis will be necessary to assess the market value of the individual tangible assets on the balance sheet. This should be accomplished line-by-line...one asset or asset group at a time.

Enterprise Value: Before we further review the assessment process, it is important to look carefully at two definitions. These are:

- **Enterprise value**
- **Invested capital**

These definitions should solidify the foundation needed to:

Picture the business. "When it's done."

Enterprise value is the market value of the business on a debt free basis. In other words, the business value as if all the capital is equity. This is the price buyer would pay for all the assets of the business. Such a buyer would then develop his or her own capital structure for the business.

The formal definition of invested capital is the total capital invested in the business. Invested capital is the interest-bearing debt in the business plus shareholders' equity. What you see here is in their simplest form these two definitions are the same. *(There may be a lot of moving parts around the edges that will be addressed separately. Professional valuators will make a distinction between Enterprise Value and Invested Capital. The difference is whether cash is retained in the business. If, however, we include only the amount of cash in Enterprise Value required to contribute to the "appropriate" level of working capital, the two definitions converge.)*

To lock in the definition of invested capital, take a look at an example that we all can relate to. Most people have had the experience of buying a house. To purchase a house at a particular price, future homeowners will provide a down payment and borrow the balance from the lender. This cash down payment is the homeowner's equity. And the borrowed balance (the mortgage) on the property is the interest-bearing debt. The invested capital in the home is the combination of those two, which of course is the price paid for the home.

The balance sheet portion of the financial statement is just that...it's a balance-d sheet. *(Left side = Right Side)* Meaning that the assets side of the ledger is equal to the liabilities and equity side of the ledger. This equation can be used to simplify and enhance the picture of the ultimate transaction.

On the assets side of the ledger are current assets and fixed assets. On the liabilities and equity ledger side are current liabilities, interest-bearing debt and equity. By applying your algebra skills, you know that you can subtract the same value from both sides of the equation and maintain the equality. In this instance let's begin by subtracting current liabilities from both sides of the ledger. That will leave only interest-bearing debt and equity on the equity and liability side.

On the asset side, we will have current assets *minus* current liabilities and fixed assets. There is a financial definition for current assets minus current liabilities. This term is important in any number of ways as the picture of the ultimate business sale is put into focus. Current assets *minus* current liabilities is the definition of **working capital**. Replacing "current assets *minus* current liabilities" with "working capital" yields the following result. We have working capital *plus* fixed assets on the asset side and interest-bearing debt and equity on the liabilities and equity side of the balance sheet.

We know that in many businesses there are assets which are not entered on the balance sheet. Brand names and any number of other intangible assets are not shown on the balance sheet. Consequently, we should add that specific group of assets to the balance sheet to complete the picture. This step results in the asset side being working capital *plus* fixed assets (tangible assets) *plus* intangible assets. In a transaction this is what is sold.

What is Sold

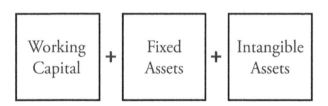

On the other side of the ledger we have interest-bearing debt plus equity. The combination of those two types of capital is "what is paid". This is the price that will ultimately be received for the business when the assets are transferred. The graphical presentation of the balance sheet algebra is provided herein for reference. The important thing is that we now know **what is to be sold** and **what is to be paid**.

What is Paid (Price)

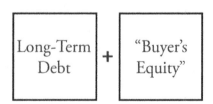

Working capital is a key component of the assets sold. In all cases working capital levels require additional analysis. In a transaction the amount of working capital transferred should be the adequate level to support operations. Excess working capital should be retained. Or any deficit to "adequate" working capital should be addressed through a reduction in the transaction price.

In most transaction structures, the seller will retain all available cash at closing and adjust the price, as required, to provide the "adequate level of working capital" agreed on in the deal. Obviously, the timing on accounts receivable collections, etc. will impact the movement of these balance sheet elements.

This is an area where financial professionals can be of great assistance. Determination of adequate working capital necessitates an effective review of the current assets and current liabilities. Such reviews require knowledge and experience. A comparison to similar business is a starting point. This is where ratio analysis can play an important role.

To employ ratio comparisons, first find the working capital ratio to sales for the most similar businesses. This ratio can be used to preliminarily assess the adequate level of working capital for the business. Once that is done, a full analysis of the cash conversion cycle will help support or modify that initial computation.

The assets to be sold include both facilities and operating assets. The facilities in most cases will be offered either for sale or lease. This approach will provide the most effectively development of a balanced transaction structure. Repair and maintenance of all these assets are essential for effective operation. This is also true for transfer preparation. The ability to neatly present all of these tangible assets, as part of the discussion of current capacity, is a positive.

To finish this preliminary step, you'll want to make a list of the balance sheet assets that will not be sold. But you do not want to stop there. To the extent possible you'll also want to list the intangible assets that have been or might contribute to future performance.

In almost all discussions concerning the sale of business the term "goodwill" is used. Unfortunately, goodwill is highly misunderstood. Goodwill is an asset. It's an asset that is created by performance. This is very important to understand so it is worth repeating.

Goodwill is an asset created by business performance!

Simply stated cash flow results of operations beyond those attributable to tangible assets create goodwill. Creating value from this asset will be an ongoing part of your business preparation.

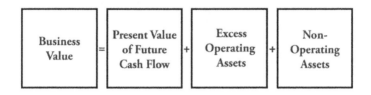

Intangible assets often drive value for strategic acquirers. Any incremental knowledge of the assets that you have might develop in this area are of great benefit in the planning process. They can become the drivers of value of the business for specific acquirers.

Other Business Assets: There are assets not specifically shown on the balance sheet. These assets include customer lists, suppliers lists, special licensed, trade names, patents, and ongoing research and development. In many situations, there are additional business assets such as: contracts, proprietary processes, operating systems, over-funded pensions, and experience ratings such as worker's compensation or unemployment. These last two directly support the employer's reputation. The stability of that key business resource... skilled employees...is a major positive attribute. Insightful business purchasers will also analyze these rating to understand the business cycles.

Assessing Readiness: Analyzing and assessing the business readiness is a quantitative and qualitative task. As noted, the balance sheet status and income statement performance analysis are an integral part of this process. Assessing and rightsizing excess and non-essential assets should be seen as incremental steps. Balance sheet positioning steps can be accomplished once effective assessment and analysis is completed. Converting assets to cash should be completed in any number of areas.

Components of working capital will be a part of the required analysis. Working capital analysis requires an understanding of:

- the average for the industry for comparison
- average for the company over a period of time
- the cash conversion cycle for the business

This information will contribute to an understanding of the required working capital for the business. The working capital levels will be used as a deal elevator in the eventual transaction. Consequently, the implications of this analysis cannot be overlooked.

Fixed asset analysis can be accomplished with your knowledge as business owner. Or, this can be done by a professional with experience and knowledge within the industry. Regardless of the approach initially chosen, these appraisals can be readdressed in the normal course of planning. Additionally, analysis regarding intangible assets can be added to complete the balance sheet picture.

Business Analysis: Knowledge is power. Your business may be more valuable than you think it is. Conversely…Your business may be more vulnerable than you think it is. Little things can make a big difference. The deep understanding of the business's risk profile, its operating characteristics, and financial leverage are critically important. As the venerable coach for the Pittsburgh Steelers, Chuck Knoll, would often say:

"When things are good, they are NOT as good as you think they are! *And* … When things are bad, they are NOT as bad as you think they are!"

It is those little things that affect risk and reward that make the difference.

Business Value: When you ask... What is the value of my business? You are really asking for two answers. The first answer is the value of the enterprise which is the price that will be paid. In terms used by financial professionals this is the value of the "invested capital" in your business. The second answer that will have more long-term meaning is: the value ultimately received as after-tax proceeds. These are the assets that can be reinvested. This measure includes the value of any excluded assets such as cash, securities, real estate, and insurance, vehicles etc. Proper professional assistance can show you the value range as well the interconnections.

Preparation: John Wooden and other great coaches will tell you the secret to success on and off the court is:

Preparation, preparation, preparation!

Just as you wouldn't schedule surgery for yourself or a family member without blood and other tests, you don't want to journey very far down this path without a professionally prepared business valuation. <u>A business valuation should be the first step in the preparation process because it provides foundational information.</u>

Happy Days
Mergers & Acquisitions

"What, you must be crazy! We thought
our business was worth three times that!"

Unfortunately, many business owners have an inflated view of the value of their company. And why not! They have put so much money and effort into it. The key to understanding and accepting an independent value estimate is to realize that "value" is going to be based on what someone else is willing to pay for the business.

A formal business valuation, prepared for planning, will effectively provide: The answer to the price question as of today (value of invested capital); the mix of capital in the value; and a solid basis for estimating the tax impact in the transaction. The business valuation should also clearly identify assets that would be excluded from the sale. A business valuation, prepared for the right purpose, is a key to initiating effective planning procedures.

Business valuation is a research project. Properly done it will provide the background information on the industry, the general economy, and the subject business. The analysis will identify alternative and substitute investments. It will analytically present the cost of capital as a measure of investment risk. And, it will provide projections to show the benefits of future ownership.

Business valuations will provide both an independent view of business operations as well as an underpinning for value planning. Specific identification of a business's value drivers should permit development of sound strategic growth and annual business plans. All of which will be needed in the preparation activity.

One of the very best books for reference on value planning is **Value Planning** *by* **Lawrence B.M. Serven**. *This book lays out the strategic and tactical steps to "build value every day"! (Other references on value planning and performance enhancement can be found at: www.MergerMentor.com under Books to Read.)*

What should you expect from the business valuation? More importantly, what should you demand? The report should be easy to read and easily understood. It should include a solid summary of the internal and external research. The report should provide detailed analysis on historic financial performance and the related trends. This information should clearly identify value drivers, and outline how the drivers provide a solid basis for future projections. The report should be easy to update and lay out a repeatable valuation process. And finally, it should be an action oriented report geared towards use in planning.

Remember What Buyers Want: A good business valuation report should provide a clear assessment of where the business is today. It should foster effective planning to get you where you want to go. You should see information on strengths and weaknesses. This will confirm the existence of critical attributes or identify areas that require attention.

Ideally, the report should clearly show that the business has:

- positive recurring cash flows
- a diversified revenue stream

- a strong balance sheet
- a believable growth story

Buyers are looking for stable, growing businesses. If there are any cracks in the foundation, that knowledge can be incorporated directly into the planning process.

Buyers want to see an owner exiting for nonbusiness reasons. (A desire to retire or step back.) They're not looking for the businesses or industries with performance problems or other issues. Mid-size businesses are like small ships on a big ocean. Buyers recognize that and the potential risk.

That is one reason they are going to demand a growth engine be in place. This knowledge is a key part of understanding what buyers want. You want to target these results when you put strategic and annual business plans in place. The tools and measures outlined in a business valuation can be put directly to work in planning.

Understanding the Research: Business valuation is all about gathering, understanding, and analyzing the facts. Whether it's the general economy, the area economy, the industry sector, or the subject business ...the process is the same. In today's environment there are tremendous external resources available to business owners and business valuators. Governments, universities, and information aggregators all provide no-cost or low-cost, high-quality inputs for valuation analysis. Industry groups, such as the national Association of Manufacturers, NFIB, specific trade associations, utility companies, bankers, and other professionals are all excellent sources of external materials.

A professional business valuator will be great in general market research. These experts will quickly understand the business's target markets, marketing methods, pricing practices, and distribution methods. One of the reasons that the valuation report has multiple uses is because this is the information needed to complete a transaction. This "intelligence" is eventually sought by business acquirers in the due diligence process.

Additional internal information regarding trained employees will all be gleaned from company reports. The is the beginning point to assess the quality and diversity of the management in place. This is a quantitative and qualitative process. Historic performance will be an indicator that the human resources are either in place or not. This internal analysis is hard work and time consuming. But it is rewarding because it provides the insights needed for value enhancements.

Information on the facilities and equipment are also all normally developed from internal documents. Knowledge on capacity utilization should come from an analysis of production reports. Similarly, the capital investments required to maintain capacity come directly from a historic review.

Valuation reports should identify operating systems or the lack thereof. This includes marketing and sales, production and delivery processes, as well as financial measures, and control systems. The financial condition of the business relative to industry peers should be effectively presented. Balance sheet and income statement analysis are only the beginning of this historic investigation.

Gross margins, which are a key point of analysis for buyers, should be tracked, analyzed and understood.

Additionally, break even points for current and projected operations should be included. Breakeven analysis is an important preliminary risk assessment measurement. *(Operating leverage positions and improvements are subjects for analysis by astute buyers.)*

Business Position: A business valuation should have an extensive SWOT analysis to maximize its usefulness. The strengths to be accentuated should be clearly documented. Weaknesses and areas requiring improvement and change should be evident. Threats to the industry and the business should be delineated along with methods of mitigation. And last, opportunities for sale and margin growth in the target market segments should be clear. These are key parts of the basis for future revenue and income estimates.

Most bankers use a specific type of report card for your business. This is comparative ratio analysis. You want your business valuator to provide the same type of ratio analysis that your bankers are using. These are useful management reporting metrics and key value assessment tools. Any good finance text should provide a list of operating ratios, leverage ratios, and financial ratios for reference. The comparative position of your business, relative to the industry, can be captured with these tools. An understanding of key ratios will be indispensable as you paint the picture of your future business. These comparative ratios will help you assess how ready the business is for sale.

Some valuators will choose to analyze as few as three years of historic financial reports. This simply is not enough. Five years is the minimum. In some cases, if it's a cyclical industry, a longer period is mandated. The preliminary financial analysis and the statistical comparisons are major parts of the basis for future estimates.

The valuator will prepare adjusted (economic) financial statements for the historic period. (These are often referred to as "normalized statements".) Both business appraisers and dealmakers should exhibit an expertise in this area. Development of this economic picture of business operations results from a line by line review and adjustment. This process is often called "normalizing" or "recasting". Regardless of the terminology, it involves a line-by-line adjustment to market value of all operating assets. It also includes removal of any non-operating assets from the balance sheet. In addition, any nonrecurring or unique occurrences uncovered in the income statement analysis will be normalized. *(All required operating expenses will be stated at market value.)* This is all part of the research and analysis process that you will find in every good business valuation report.

What you should see within the report: The business valuation report should clearly provide the following information in a readable, easily understandable manner:

- Determination of excess or deficit in operating assets
- Identification and separation of non-operating assets
- Projection of future cash flows and "funded CAP-X"
- Estimate of invested capital (FMV Price Estimate)
- Cost (tax) basis for assets to be transferred
- Value estimate for tangible assets to be transferred
- Value estimate for intangible assets portion of price
- Information for allocation on form 8594 (and implication)
- Strengths to build on; weaknesses to mitigate
- Risk drivers (to be understood and addressed)

- Value drivers (to be measured and put to use)
- Tools and templates for iteration of scenarios in planning
- Market analysis and growth rate support
- Identification of under-utilized tangible and intangible assets

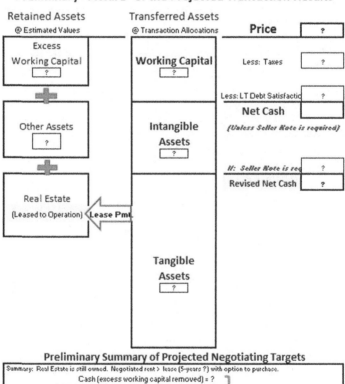

Preliminary "Picture" of the Projected Transaction Results

Preliminary Summary of Projected Negotiating Targets

Summary: Real Estate is still owned. Negotiated rent > lease (5-years ?) with option to purchase.

Cash (excess working capital removed) = ?
Cash net received from transaction price paid = ?
Seller Note with negotiated terms in the amount = ? **Il amounts subject to negotiations**
Investment Assets (Marketable Securities) retained = ?
Cash Value of retained life insurance = ?

Existing Value of Real Estate Plus: ?

Please refer to the graphic summary of the primary information in a business valuation for further understanding of this "picture". This is what you should learn as part of the review.

You should be able to fill in all the blanks (?) on the chart to summarize your valuation results on one page. This is your current position.

Note: The final price realized may be different than the estimated invested capital value due to the motivations and relative negotiating strengths of the buyers and sellers in any specific transaction.

The 1% Solution: Unfortunately consistent use of business valuations for assessment and planning are not part of every owner's current processes. Business valuations are most often prepared for state or gift filings and/or as part of one of the dismal Ds, divorce. One can argue that the best use of a business valuation is for long-term planning.

Chris Mercer, a highly recognized valuation professional, has written a report that has important observations in it. (You can read it directly at: http://chrismercer.net/one-percent-solution-examined/.) Chris argues that management of 401(k)s and other assets entrusted to wealth management professionals typically incur an annual cost of approximately 1%. Assets with less than $1 million in value might have costs for management closer to the 1.5% range. Assets over $5 million may have costs reduced to the .75% area. Chris's assertion is that business owners should similarly assess and manage their most important business asset, their privately-held business. Expenditure of similar amounts on private company value management can potentially have a much greater benefit.

Beyond Chris's message to prompt action, there is the well-known principle that is used throughout management. This principle is:

What gets measured gets done.

The business valuation measures value and provides a method to project future value. It is this assessment measurement process that yields the real benefits. So please consider having an annual or bi-annual valuation prepared for your business starting right now.

It's the business valuation, properly prepared, that will prompt and keep a focus on the current and future performance. In addition, the valuation will provide an assessment of the tax impact in the transaction and other information useful in early estate planning. Putting a valuation to work in the business preparation process is a minimal step towards assembling the needed knowledge and the tools for action.

"Based on our calculations and years of hard work,
Molly and I believe the price of our business
should be based on our revenues right about there!"

Once completed, you will wonder why no one outlined the benefits for you before now.

How to Find a <u>Certified</u> Business Valuator (Appraiser)

There are a number of professional organizations that train and certify business valuators (appraisers) with a focus on privately-held small and middle market businesses. If you do not have a current advisor who can provide a direct referral to a business valuator with whom they have personal experience, you can find a **certified professional** through one of these organizations:

American Society of Appraisers (ASA)
(www.appraisers.org)

Institute of Business Appraisers (IBA)
(www.go-iba.org)

National Association of Certified Valuators
and Analysts (NACVA)
(www.nacva.com)

If you operate a small, main street business, the ISBA focuses specifically on that particular market segment.

International Society of Business Analysts
(www.intlbca.com)

Chapter 4

Getting the Business Ready

(Value Enhancement)

Making the Difference: It takes effective and consistent actions to improve the performance of a business. It also takes time. With that in mind, it is absolutely important to have a strategic plan to follow. If your business has not developed a pattern of formal planning over the years, now is the time to start. Experience shows that the best way to develop a strategic plan is to engage a skilled facilitator to lead the process.

Preparing a Strategic Plan: There is nothing magic about preparing a strategic plan. An experienced strategic planner will help you ask and answer the right questions in the right order. When completed, the plan should clearly answer the following questions:

- What should the business be doing?

  (Identify strategies and opportunities)

- How should the business be doing it?

  (Develop projects and tactics)

- When should things be done?

  (Assess and sequence input/output timing)

- Who will do all these things?

  (Assemble internal and external required resources)

- Why should we do certain things in a certain way?

  (Lock-in the reasoning)

The larger question before you begin may be: Why create a strategic plan at all? The answer to that question should drive the entire process. To get the best results start by listing the interim and long-term benefits that you want from the planning process.

Let's look at an example of what is possible. In one of our engagements we were able to outline several steps for management to take in order to improve financial performance. They followed the advice and increased gross margins by just over 3% and concurrently reduced overhead costs by more than 2%. In addition, by focusing on some key statistics, they were able to increase inventory turns by 50%. These changes nearly doubled net income and reduced the total required inventory by over 35%. With more cash flow and renewed energy, the owners went on to increase sales and more than doubled the value of their business. This transition took almost two years to complete, but it positioned the business for an attractive sale...later when the timing was right! *(With focus and effort you can gain these types of benefits too!)*

Once you're done with the initial planning, again list the benefits that you anticipate from the plan. These benefits may include management development, cash flow improvement, and acceleration of risk mitigation. But you want to go well beyond these more general benefits and get very specific. You want to quantify the performance improvement benefits in dollars and ease of operation. This list of benefits will become the reasons for you and your management team to make hard decisions. Continuously referring to the list will help you fast-track the development of your business. Focusing on these benefits will get you...and keep you...on track.

Japanese proverb:
Having a vision
without action
is nothing
but a day dream,
and taking action
without a vision
is a nightmare!

Sound, strategic thinking is very important to the create results that you seek. The strategies chosen will have the controlling influence on the plan's success. It should be remembered that strategies focus on effectiveness, which is doing the right things! Superior planning should provide for both effective and efficient actions. It takes continuous strategic and tactical activities to deliver timely results.

Strategic plan preparation requires application of knowledge and experience. Inputs in this phase flow from the research provided in the formal business valuation. That process is not all-inclusive, but it's a beginning. Truly understanding: Where the business is…is the first step in determining the answers to key planning questions.

The formal planning process, especially if it's led by an experienced professional, will establish business goals and objectives. Although some goals may be qualitatively stated, it's the quantitative measures that will ultimately drive the process. These goals and objectives should be clearly understood and integrated into a picture of the business in the future. Developing strategies to realize goals are the basis for effective plan formulation. It's the timing and sequence of the strategic steps that permit the business to reach its objectives. This is the process that yields the real value. All strategies should be tested and retested before implementation. Choice of an inappropriate strategy can have a debilitating effect on the business.

Once the strategies are in place and understood, projects should be created to implement the strategy. <u>Such projects should specifically detail who will do what, when, and why.</u> In addition, the resources required should be fully understood by all involved. The ultimate power of the plan comes from the combination of effective strategies and detailed project planning. Not all plans are perfect. To keep on track to reach the stated goals and objectives, a feedback loop is indispensable. Reporting systems should quickly and effectively identify adjustments necessary to ultimately reach the target.

The term "value engineering" is often used relative to the strategic planning process. This term is relatively simple to define: it is the planning and actions required to improve performance to fill the valuation gap. This is the gap between the value of the business today and the owners' ultimate objectives. A part of this value engineering process planning should focus on reduction of actual or perceived risks. The stated purpose of the plan will normally focus on operating changes and growth to increase financial performance. Such growth oriented projects should fit into the planning horizon set by the business owner. This timeline may be relatively short term, i.e. one or two years, or it may be five years or longer.

The business valuation analysis should permit you to determine what is required to reach the stated objectives. Each value enhancement project must deliver a measurable improvement. These benefits must stay in balance with the financial resources committed to the plan.

© Michael H Marks

ACADEMY
Talent Agency

"Do you have any good actors that can fill in as
key employees on Tuesday morning?
I have a buyer coming to look at my business!"

If the internal management skills in place are not sufficient to fill the valuation gap, external resources should be sought. These are specifically the professionals necessary to accelerate the process to assure that the business is ready sooner. An important part of this work may include hiring, training, and managing of the right talented and motivated employees.

Growth Planning: Within the planning process, major customers and customer groups should be identified. This is where the revenue is going to come from to obtain the desired growth. When these targeted customers and customer groups are growing at an accelerated pace, the business should passively benefit. Recurring growth of this nature should be sought to establish a solid foundation for future projections.

To get the most out of the underlying analysis, put yourself in the position of the business acquirer. As a buyer you will want to review the most important products and services. And you will want to know they were thoroughly analyzed as part of the planning process. What is sold today may be different than what will be sold tomorrow. This knowledge and the associated plans are exactly what astute buyers will be seeking. A deep understanding of the market place...as it is and as it is expected to be...should be evident in the strategies chosen.

Once the preliminary plans are in place, accountability for performance must be clearly established and accepted by management. Whether it is sales growth or customer diversification, management must implement plans to reach the objectives. Similarly, any required margin expansion and income growth must be accepted measurements of management's performance. The related improvements in the management team and the systems in place should clearly be discrete objectives.

The portions of the plan that deal with competition and other external factors should be set up for continuous updating. Buyers will expect to see real-time market knowledge acquisition systems. Any risks associated with other external factors should be delineated and diminished as possible. The key to get the most value is to keep an eye on the value drivers and risk contributors identified in the business valuation. Understanding and using the company's competitive advantages is a major part of eliminating external friction that might slow progress.

Planning Analysis: To achieve the anticipated valuation results, it is advisable to: state and restate the three most important actions. These focused actions are going to be found in the projects with the 20/80 attributes that we're all familiar with. Everyone involved should expect and believe that these actions will deliver the stated benefits. Documenting the anticipated progress along a rigid timeline can setup the measurements required to prompt critical decisions. By focusing on the high-value strategies, management should be able to easily frame 3 to 5 value-enhancing projects.

Value enhancing projects should lead to consistent tactical actions. To do this, it is imperative to establish who is responsible for each step. Agreement on the timeline, key milestones, resources requirements, reporting, and the feedback process is what delivers results. As noted earlier, a clear statement of the benefits to be delivered by specific programs will help maintain focus and commitment.

Strategic Plan Summary: The formal strategic planning report should be something that management refers to on a continuous basis. A one-page plan summary should be prepared and used to enhance communications. This one-page summary should concisely state the top three objectives. Show what they are and when they MUST be accomplished. This one-page summary should outline the basic strategies adopted to reach the objectives. This is the **"How will we do it?"** answer for all involved.

This one-page strategic plan summary should list the current year's major projects. As the plan progresses over time, these projects should be replaced or reaffirmed. These are the **"Who"** and **"When"** answers. Management must commit annually to this type of business plan. This one-page summary should clearly state the benefits of reaching the foremost objectives. This is the **"Why do it?"** answer.

Thoughts to remember:
The very best way to predict the future
is to create it!

All senior managers should be reviewing this one-page summary every day. There's nothing that slows progress in a value-engineering project more than lack of focus. This simple step of reviewing the one-page strategic plan goes a long way toward reducing this ever present risk to the plan. Management should be measuring results on a weekly basis for the projects on which they have direct responsibility. For the higher level objectives, monthly or quarterly reporting should be sufficient. This reporting regiment should provide timely feedback to foster appropriate plan adjustments.

By nature of their function, managers focus on budgets and financial results. This is excellent as long as the right things are being measured, at the right time, and in the right way. By focusing on a limited number of measures, management should develop the insights needed to drive actions, gain additional knowledge, and ensure employee engagement in the process.

Continuous Learning: The annual business plan should include provisions to promote continuous learning by all employees. Employees should be encouraged to establish and use systems so they can go from insights to usable knowledge. The organization should be developed and changed to improve effectiveness. All employees should be empowered to improve efficiency. Everything necessary should be done to ensure that employees perceive operating changes that enhance effectiveness and efficiency as REQUIRED actions.

An excellent book to read and to recommend to any management team is **Strategic Learning** *by:* **Willie Pietersen**. *This book delivers on the tagline "How to be smarter than your competition and to turn key insights into a competitive advantage."*

Continuous improvement of data collection, quality, and timing should be the minimum requirement. <u>All reporting should be reduced to the minimum information required for decision making</u>. In this regard, management should be continuously assessing key customer relationships. This is the only way to ensure the business is moving in the right direction and positioned for the desired growth. Once this culture of continuous improvement is in place, it is important to allow for normal variances. You do not want to tinker with working systems and employees who are exercising judgment based on sound criteria.

<u>Buyers will be looking for repeatable processes in the business</u>. All plans should include provisions to systematize all functioning processes. This includes marketing and sales, human resources, administration, as well as the primary operations to deliver products and services. There are many ways to show evidence that these systems are in place and working. ISO certification is just one simple example. Low employee turnover is normally clear evidence of excellent hiring and training processes. Whatever the process is, there should be, at a minimum, skeleton documentation in place. Such documentation provides a basis for process improvement.

Ultimately the same performance that enhances value delivers evidence that the business has sound processes. Buyers will be looking for operations in which the systems accentuate the strengths of the business. If only minimal changes are required in this area, an astute buyer will recognize that they can focus more time on strategies for future growth. These systems are the foundation for easy scalability that will provide an additional intangible asset for transfer.

Yield Measurement: A part of all strategic and business planning is prudent capital budgeting. A very disciplined approach to assure required "returns on all investment" (ROI) will deliver the best results. The hurdle rate for capital investment returns can be gleaned from the business valuation. The discount rate used in the income approach is the baseline rate for the cost of capital. Use of this rate in ROI analysis may require modification. To account for the unknowns and other risks in specific projects, this baseline cost of capital can and should be adjusted.

Specific (CAP-X) capital investment plans depend on the timing for a planned future ownership transition. Clear understanding of the timing of the cash flow benefits from any such investments is needed to make these decisions. The cash flow contribution from specific investments may not be evident early enough to warrant an investment. By plotting value-added investments on a timeline, the astute business owner should be able to properly temper CAP-X decisions.

The other area that requires careful analysis is human resources. Specific measurements for return on effort (ROE) are very important. No business should put plans in place that require this critical resource to approach exhaustion. Economically measuring these returns as part of performance reviews is an important step to maintain both progress and appropriate balance.

Most Important Resource: Good business owners will almost always state that their most important assets are their employees. We all know this to be true at some level. Any knowledgeable purchaser of a business will certainly focus a portion of their analysis on the employees. Buyers are going to specifically look at the operating relationships employees have with the business. Buyers want to see the employees' specific personal and business connections. These strong relationships foster longevity, low turnover, and a commitment to the ultimate customer.

Buyers are going to look for any concentration of management responsibilities. Good, enhanced value planning should address these issues. Specifically, steps should be taken to spread out key responsibilities. These include operating responsibilities and key customer relationships. In addition, any concentration of experience and skills within the workforce should be addressed. It certainly may not be possible to make these adjustments in all cases. But it is unquestionably desirable to understand the situation and how it may impact an acquirer's assessment of risk.

Managers Metrics and Structure: The short list of what to look for in management development would be as follows: operational functions should be handled by multiple managers with appropriate backups; there should be more than three top line managers reporting to the owner; customer relationships should be handled by multiple managers; and vendor relationships should also be handled by multiple managers.

If annual sales revenues are developed and controlled by one employee in any significant manner, it may be a critical issue for a business purchaser. Specifically, no salesperson or manager should be responsible for any more than 20 or 25% of sales revenue. Market knowledge and customer knowledge should be broadly dispersed. Someone beyond the owner should be capable of handling problems and issues with lead customers and vendors. Metrics below these levels increase perceived risk of repeatability and achievement of forecasts.

Management development and restructuring should be part of a natural process. Spreading responsibilities among managers for customers, vendors, and key parts of the operation should come with growth. By carefully integrating such management transitions into the growth plans, appropriate opportunities can be developed. Properly developed incentives and overall compensation should fit within the projected budgets. A business owner should act with caution in this area to ensure that there is no short-term or long-term undesirable performance impact!

There is little value in diversifying management responsibilities if the management team is not producing good results! Astute buyers will work hard to determine:

- How management has and will react to trends and changes
- How effective is management's customer focus
- How management produced growth to increase value

Given that the ultimate objective is "readying the business for sale," all of these management issues should be included in the planning. All existing contractual relationships should be reviewed. A clear understanding of current and future confidentiality issues and their potential impact should be sought. In addition, the need for any new contractual relationships or other retention plans should be soberly assessed. Resource planning in this area should include risk assessment and mitigation actions!

Value Enhancement Delivered: Bridging the gap from where the value of the business is today to where you want to be in the future requires business performance improvement. Regardless of the planning horizon, it is important to focus on a few high impact areas. As stated and restated, it is paramount to engage employees in the overall process. Rigorously working on the plans with the management team and then acting quickly on feedback are the minimum requirements for success.

Understanding of the value drivers comes from the business valuation. This information is a direct input into planning. Many of these value drivers are measured as percentages. Businesses essentially run on percentages...and so do acquirer's assessments. As an example: you might look at what two or three increased percentage points of gross margin might mean over the next 3 to 5 years. *(This may be as simple as an analysis of what a marginal price increase might do. Or it could be more complex.)*

Customer Development: Growth in free cash flow is the ultimate objective of the value enhancement processes. However, if the growth in revenue results in additional customer concentration, there may not be any long-term value enhancement. Professional investors are going to be looking for businesses that have no single customer with greater than 15% of sales. Similarly, these business investors will be seeking companies that have less than 50% of sales from their top 8 to 10 customers.

Concentration of sales in an industry or a narrow sector of an industry may also be a negative factor for an acquirer. Diversification of customers and sales certainly will reduce risk and enhance salability. As part of the planning process, new customer development and other steps to change these metrics over time should be emphasized. Similarly, any product dominance should be soberly evaluated and steps taken to add diversification. These risk evaluations should be inputs to the top projects. Risk reduction steps should be the action-oriented output from the strategic and business planning efforts.

Balance Sheet Positioning Power: One of the central outputs from the final business valuation was the analysis of working capital. The "right sizing" information regarding working capital is a direct input to a good planning process. Improvement of the accounts receivable collection cycle, collection of bad debts, and/or recognition of appropriate write-offs should be the focus within a project to improve the balance sheet. Similarly, improvement of the inventory turnover and adjustment of the product mix held enhances the underlying components of working capital. Sale of obsolete or slowly moving inventory can free cash for redeployment to enhance customer service.

Segregation of non-operating assets or removing them from the balance sheet is part of the business readiness process. Sale of any excess current or fixed assets will also improve the picture of the business from this perspective. This effort to reposition the assets on the balance sheet should be integrated into the performance and growth planning.

Removal, to the extent possible, of personal assets such as vehicles, airplanes, etc. should be carefully accomplished. Life insurance policies, if they are not required for lending, may be distributed. Similarly, investment assets that are liquid should be distributed within the normal bounds of prudent tax planning. All of these steps should be part of the overall business readiness process.

On the liabilities side of the balance sheet, any efforts to tighten up payables, which impacts the working capital computation, will be viewed in a positive light. Assets freed up and converted to cash can be used to pay down lines of credit or to otherwise reduce term debt. These balance sheet changes will reduce the financial leverage and the related risks. Elimination of personal accounts such as officer's loans or other such liabilities is always helpful when preparing for an ownership transition.

If at all possible, you should discuss moving to an "audited statement" with your CPA. There may be some added costs, but the payback can be notable. Lenders appreciate audited statements. And buyers certainly place a lot more weight on such financial information as they move through early analysis phases and into due diligence.

"Both of these businesses are listed for $1 million. One makes $400,000 per year, and the other makes $90,000. And you want to know which one I am interested in?"

Remember: As you, the business owner, engage in readying the business for sale, it is important to remember: **What gets sold!** and …**What gets paid!** and… **Why!** The ultimate selling price must be justified and competitive in the market place. With that knowledge, you can secure numerous advantages by carefully and completely preparing the business for sale....Now! Always remembering:

Price is
what you receive.
Value is
what you deliver!

Chapter 5

The Hardest Part
of the Answer

Remember the Dismal Ds: Use this grim reality to develop motivation to begin and to persevere. It is massively important for you, the business owner, to be highly motivated in this phase of preparation. Deep personal reflections are always hard. None more so than those involving a life's work...as important as your business. So some additional reflection on the Disraeli quote is warranted:

Action does not guarantee happiness, But... there is no happiness without action!

If you want to beat the odds...you want to be ready regardless of the event or the timing. You want to begin and keep moving the business and yourself toward a posture of readiness. You want to be ready for an unplanned ownership transition. Hopefully, that will not occur. In which case you will position the business and yourself for an optimally planned transition. This is the timetable you are preparing.

Picture Yourself: Begin this phase of preparation by picturing yourself without the business. What would you do each day? Can you see yourself in that picture fully separated from your business?

To start, you want to determine if you have sufficient interest outside the business. This can be anything from social activities, sports activities, charitable work, or other business interests. If you cannot quickly make a list of these potential activities, it's a good indication that you are engulfed in your business. This is not abnormal. But when you are planning to separate yourself from the business it's an issue.

As an example, earlier in our intermediary work, we completed a transaction for a client. Everyone was happy. The deal worked for all involved. Management was in place and the seller only had an "on call" consulting arrangement. It all seemed right. Or at least that is what we thought until I received a call from the client's wife about ten days after closing. She said: You have to help me. All he does is follow me around the house…into the kitchen, the laundry room, or outside.

This was a man who worked seven days a week for over thirty-five years on and in his business. He had never developed other interests. It was a learning experience for us and a problem that we felt that we needed to solve for the client. After a couple meetings to "move toward the problem," I asked: Would you like to have a part-time job? The answer was immediate...YES. So several weeks later, we arranged for him to start work three days a week with a non-competing business, and he accepted the assignment to find new interests on the other two days. It worked and taught us the importance of addressing these matters earlier in the process.

So, you can see the importance of looking at yourself in this way now. It is usually helpful to take a few minutes to figure out with whom you would spend more time. Ask your spouse or a confidant to assist you. As you both assess and picture this future, you should see it as a freeing benefit. Hopefully, the people you would spend more time with would add joy to every day.

Regarding the business, there are two key questions that you should ask and answer. They are:

What part of the business would you miss? *And...* What part of the business would you <u>not</u> miss?

Clearly identifying what's important to you in your daily business activities will help determine your readiness for change. This simple first step should help you begin to see what you need to do to make that future picture a reality. We all appreciate people we work with in our business. That's not what we are talking about here. We are discussing the specific things you do that you will miss if you are not working in or on your business each day.

Conversely, developing a list of the things you will not miss on a daily basis should serve as a motivator. Every position, including leading a business, involves activities that at times are difficult. What we are looking for in this area are not those unique challenges. You want to identify the recurring daily, weekly, or monthly tasks that you are not going to miss.

Ideally, this list should serve as a planning tool to transfer some of those responsibilities to other managers. To the extent that is possible, there should be an immediate benefit to you personally. You will have eliminated some of these tasks and gained time to devote to planning and added concentration on the business readiness process.

It's important to also ask and answer: What other changes would you make? These can be both business

© Michael H. Marks

"Gee honey, if you feel that way, maybe it's time to sell the business!"

activity changes and/or personal pattern changes. This list may be very short or nonexistent. Or it may be the formalization of thoughts you have had for a long time. In either case the result should help you take the needed actions.

Emotional readiness: Ask yourself if you're emotionally ready for a new role in life? If this question is met with silence, ask your spouse or confidant. Under the assumption that this is a person who knows you best, the answer can prompt a productive conversation.

This is the background for the canvas you are painting of the future. Answers in this area are normally hard and take time.

Professional advisors to owners of midsize businesses generally agree on one thing in this area. Many of them have found that owners who have not planned a transition by the time they reach age 65 are struggling with emotional detachment. These owners may still have great joy in operating their business day-to-day. The difficulty comes from the potential disruption that may occur due to this lack of planning. Without effective planning, the future transition, when it occurs, may dramatically affect both the business and family.

The retention of the business by an older owner may be accompanied by sub-optimal investment in the business. This is a natural result of the owner's change in risk taking. Older owners become more risk adverse. They act much different from the time when the business was being built.

Once a financial plateau is reached, risk tolerance can change. Instead of focusing on business growth, the focus may change to one of current lifestyle maintenance. Some businesses suffer from this more than others. Businesses lose some of their vibrancy in this way especially if more driven managers choose to depart. Additionally, customers seeking new products may be forced to add vendors or make a complete change. All of these occurrences unfortunately move the business away from readiness for an ownership transition.

Personal considerations: As I just noted, one of the things to assess is your level of interest in business development. Growth plans are normally accompanied by some level of risk. At times, however, a greater risk can develop from a lack of interest in fostering normal business change and growth patterns.

You may be fully engaged in growth plans and development today. You may not be as involved at some time in the future. Measuring and understanding where you are today relative to where you want to be is vitally important. Measurements will help you move forward with your plans. And assessing your readiness for a transition will help create the comfort needed to reduce your emotional attachment.

Our personal energies certainly move in cycles. The question to ask is: Do you have the energy to easily maintain the necessary focus on the business? Do you expect to be able to sustain this energy level for a period of time? Take a look for current signs of what you do and how you do it compared to your past activities. You may be better focused today than when you were less experienced. By starting the process to monitor yourself in this area, you will be demonstrably adding to your readiness quotient. Whatever you do...don't forget these words from a great, great philosopher.

> If you wait until
> it is too late...
> It is...too late!
>
> *Quote by Yogi*

Outside Interests: Your current list of outside interests may be short. If so, it may be time for you to add to this list. This is a small step in preparation for your personal transition from the business. You can add a new interest or expand an existing interest. These outside interests may cover a very broad range.

A very wise man once said: if we are fortunate, we are able to spend one third of our lives learning, one third of our lives earning, and one third of our lives giving back. Most successful business owners never truly stop learning. So this simple division into thirds is not a black and white picture. It does, however, prompt productive thought on what interest you have or may want to have outside of your business.

There may be things in your community that you can do that others cannot. If you can find them, your contribution will not only be greatly appreciated, but it will also be rewarding to you. Such activities may be part of a local charity or may be as an official in the local government. Every organization from the Salvation Army to the school board can benefit from experienced managers. Finding the "future fit" should be part of your objectives.

The Service Corps of Retired Executives (SCORE) might be an organization to consider. On a less formal basis, there may be a number of smaller businesses that could gain from your advice. This could be as a member of the Board of Directors or in some consulting capacity. You may or may not choose to be an investor in these businesses. Once you start thinking about these other potential interests you may find that there is a level of excitement and new energy. Welcoming this new focus is part of the prescription needed for a successful transition.

© Michael H Marks

**"Are you sure the business can't live without you ---
or is it that YOU can't live without the business?"**

Commitment: Progress in the process of personal readiness will come from a determination to proceed. If you know you are not emotionally prepared, take little steps to resolve those issues. It may take time. Just as it may take time to have the business as ready as you would like it to be. These can and should be parallel paths for you and the business. Optimally you should be prepared to let go as part of management development. To the extent you become less essential to daily operations you should be adding to the readiness of the business. As you become more prepared by transferring responsibilities, the business should simultaneously become more saleable.

Risk Profile: You must soberly assess how indispensable you are to the business's success...now and in the future. Can you take vacations without continuous business communications? Are your top customers your customers or customers of the business? Is their relationship with you the defining element? These and many other operational questions must be asked and answered.

These are questions that a potential acquirer of your business is going to ask. They are part of your...and ultimately the buyers'...overall risk assessment. We know a buyer's risk adjusted rate of return is going to directly affect the value that they will pay. Mitigation of this management concentration risk will increase the price you may ultimately negotiate from an experienced buyer.

Very few business owners have a position description for themselves. They are the CEO and much more. One good step is to find a good position description template and develop your own (CEO) position description. This position description should identify responsibilities and accountabilities. Repetitive tasks, skills, and experience needed to succeed in the job should be defined. Once you have accomplished this, you will be ready for the next step. You can then augment it with deeper thinking in this area.

You want to determine how you can change your role without impacting future performance. As an example: How can you get "Old Joe," your best customer, to meet with your sales manager instead of you? As you carefully reduce your responsibilities and recurring tasks, you can strengthen management. This added management strength will impact a buyer's risk calculation. Without these steps, you don't know how a buyer may incorporate your departure into their analysis. They may assert that the business is going to lose half of the revenue from "Old Joe" without you. They may not communicate this directly, but you will be aware of it from the price ceiling they develop.

As part of this process of assessing your role and responsibilities, you will want to consider how long you would like to stay…after the sale. Depending on the type of transaction, this may be the lead operating role. Or after a transition period, it may be as an essential consultant and advisor. Knowing what you would like to do, post-sale, is the first step in preparing for the negotiation. Make no mistake, CEO continuity will be required as part of the business transfer.

If you haven't fully reduced your critical roles, it may be important to stay with the business to satisfy the buyer's concerns.

What you must be careful not to do is to clone yourself and replicate the risk. As you transfer direct responsibilities you will want to assign them to multiple managers. You should use position descriptions as key tools in this endeavor. You want to review and re-review your plans before you act. The first priority is to maintain and improve business performance. Second priority is diversification of management responsibility. Nothing good will be accomplished by assigning responsibilities to someone who is either not ready or not willing to accept them. Reducing one set of risks by introducing others is not going to add to the readiness of the business. Or in your personal readiness for a transition.

Family Members: One of the great things about many privately-held businesses is the opportunities to work with and develop family members. It is also the potential source of difficulty in planning an ownership transfer. (In Chapter 6 we are going to work through a preference matrix, as separate steps, to help you judge that part of your readiness for a sale. By applying that same tool to family scenarios, this can help see this more clearly.) What we want to determine are the strengths and weaknesses introduced by family involvement in the business. Part of this work is to realistically assess the level of long-term interest the family members have in the business.

It's important to focus on the contributions from family members in the sales process and other parts of the operation. These individuals may play a very important part in any buyer's assessment of risks. They may be key parts of the management diversification plan that you put in place. Family members also may provide important leadership for the future of the business post sale. If buyers are comfortable with family members remaining as part of the management team and believe they will continue to contribute, their presence will help in the transition.

© Michael H Marks

"What do you mean you don't want to take over the family business? You go to your room right now mister, you are grounded!"

If the buyers believe that key family members may depart from the business, that fact may introduce an insurmountable risk. <u>These risks can be mitigated with contractual relationships and non-compete agreements.</u> Understanding what family members would like to do in the future is an important part of the overall assessment. To be ready for a sale, you must have your family members fully prepared. Determination of their future desires and personal plans should be part of your early analysis. You will need these 'inputs" to begin to picture what the business will look like in the future.

Succession Planning: One of the best ways to strengthen management and to uncover both family and other senior managers' future expectations is with formal succession planning. This process can and should be started in a normal manner. It can be done with or without an experienced facilitator. But, in a lot of cases, the experience a professional brings to the process can be decisive.

The succession process itself is not a mystery. It involves a diagnosis of current management's strengths and weaknesses overlaid on the future needs of the business. The question then is: Does the business have the managers in place to execute a succession plan without major adjustments? If not, then a chunk of the process is to recruit, train, and support additional managers as indicated.

The succession plan should support the strategic plans and the annual business plans. The succession outline should drive the transition while fully supporting other plans. For you and the business to be ready, experienced management must be in place. Also, for you and the business to be ready, these managers must have proven abilities to execute the growth plans.

The most effective succession plans usually involve the CEO moving into a planning position. This should permit the CEO, owner, (YOU) to spend 25 to 50% of their time on strategic issues. This focus should help reduce direct customer responsibilities and contacts. The slow but consistent delegation of responsibilities should be a driver of overall improvement of the management team.

Broader Family Considerations: The earlier discussion concerning family members and the business is only the first step in that area. If family members in the business will not, or should not, be part of the future business plans, then there is immediate work required! These family members may be comfortable seeking other employment, or they may look to you to help them buy another noncompeting business. Knowing what is expected by all family members is essential in the planned allocation of your overall resources.

If family members are not working in the business, it may be important to provide assistance for them in the future. This may be direct funding of the purchase of a smaller business or support for additional college or related plans. Or it may be funding of college for their children to reduce these future obligations. With the cost of education rising, these are major considerations.

You do not want to be diligently working on your readiness for a transaction without equal consideration of your family's work plans. <u>This is not something you want to make assumptions about!</u> Your family may be fully ready for the personal transition. Or they may have no desire to change what they're doing for quite some time. Knowing this will not only impact your personal planning but also the planning horizon.

Most business owners have had some interaction with financial planners. Discussion typically relates to pension plans at work or through specific wealth management programs. If you have not engaged a professional to develop a personal financial plan for you...now is the time to do so.

One of the key outputs from this planning process will be to show the "potential resource gap." This is the difference between your personal resources outside the business and your future needs. This is the gap that can be filled by the sale of your business. The required after-tax contribution from the business sale will become your value target. This analysis will help you determine what you need to achieve in the business sale. The business valuation is an additional information component. The value gap is a direct input into the value engineering work plans. If the business value today is not sufficient to support your personal plans, the answer is *to increase the value.*

Estate Plans: Estate plans should flow directly from financial plans and other personal considerations. Early discussions with an experienced legal advisor will lay the foundation needed in this area. Estate plans have major financial implications as well as multiple family reflections. Payment of estate taxes, funding of trusts, and fulfilling charitable and other objections should be clearly addressed within the estate plan. Funding of portions of the plan with life insurance may help optimize the results. All of this work, and it is work, requires competent professional assistance. Early efforts in this area will help by providing information for use in business and personal planning. One thing to remember is that the estate plan can and should be updated at regular intervals or immediately when things change. There is a feedback loop between all the plans that must be fully appreciated and respected.

"Detailed" Cash Planning: Your financial planner and your estate planner should directly address how all of the cash will flow in the future. Your personal investments outside the business can go from a reserve posture to consumption. Proceeds, net of taxes, from the sale of your business should significantly augment your existing outside investments. Life insurance policies with cash values are also a potential cash source to be applied to your personal plans. To the extent that these policies are in place to pay estate taxes, those commitments must be understood. All of these resources and liquidity generators should be integrated into your plans.

Pensions have a slightly different characteristic in that proceeds are fully taxable in most cases. These taxes are at ordinary income rates. If you and/or your spouse are the beneficiaries of a defined benefit plan that cash flow, net of taxes, will be your retirement foundation. 401(k) plans, SEPs, or IRAs should be key elements in your financial plan. Your financial planner will probably advise you to withdraw no more than 5% annually from these plans.

These cash flows should all be clearly delineated in your financial plan. The uses of funds should be well understood by both you and your spouse. Security for you and your spouse should come from highly stable future cash flows.

It is often instructive to make a list of all the assets that you have and to put them into two columns. One column is for assets that require cash to maintain (homes, camps, etc.). The other column is for assets that provide cash to you on a regular basis. These all may be seen as "investments" but they have dramatically different characteristics. This enlightening procedure will help you determine which assets you want to maintain in the future and which ones you may want to sell or gift.

The separation of these assets into cash generating and cash consuming categories is the major step. This process may, however, surface differences between you and your spouse regarding what to retain and what to dispose of in the long term. Your financial planner may be the best person to help you reach a resolution in these areas of discussion.

Once you've made the preliminary determinations of your retirement plans (estate and financial plans) and the variable sources and uses of cash... any gap should be clear. This is the gap that your business sale can and should fill. By estimating the differential cash flow required from additional invested assets, you should be able to compute the after-tax target for the sale of your business. It is typically instructive to analyze use of the resources provided by the business. By computing the cash contribution at 4%, 6%, and 8%, as a return on the reinvested assets, you can estimate the amount of added resources required.

The projected cash flow may be well beyond your computed requirements for retirement. That is what you are working for. This is your money, and you can do with it as you want. You want to be using it for your family and for your personal enjoyment. To help assure you can do this without regret comes from planning.

If this simple computation doesn't give you the comfort desired, go back and diligently work on financial plans and plans to increase the value of the business. Planning horizons may need to change. Strategies may need to change. Timelines may need to be accelerated. It's up to you to do the planning and re-planning necessary to reach the goal that you have outlined for yourself in this process. Knowing now what you want to accomplish certainly makes a great difference.

Just as in any good planning process, you want to create and use a formal feedback loop to accelerate

Be **S A F E** thru Planning

business preparation. This requires that there are out-puts from personal planning and essential inputs for business growth and development! You can increase your readiness by gaining comfort with your business, financial, and estate plans. All of the interim planning steps along the way add value!

A good way to remind yourself of the interfaces between your various plans can combine to make you SAFE. This acronym should resonate for you since in the end all of the work and planning is really focused on just that. Making you and your family SAFE and SECURE. The risks from being SAFE come from delays and deferrals of action.

> # Warning:
> ## The dates in your calendar are closer than they appear!

All of your planning must work together to reach the objectives within the planning horizon. After you've done the re-planning and created a new picture... Analyze it! Reassess all your family considerations. Double check your position and your spouse's position regarding plans. Assure yourself that the detailed cash flow required will be available to maintain and improve your lifestyle. And finally... relook at yourself and your personal readiness. It likely has improved dramatically though this effort.

Chapter 6

Exercise Helps

We all know how important good nutrition and regular exercise are to good personal health. That truism cannot be overlooked as you prepare yourself to transfer the ownership of your business. The preparation and the ultimate execution of a transfer plan will require both focus and a good measure of personal energy. The recognition of this fact is important to assure that you don't stall along the timeline. If you've already established good health and wellness habits, that's great. If not, it's fundamentally important that you include changes in this area as an early objective.

There's a different exercise, however, that will help ready both you and the business for a planned ownership change. It is an exercise in THINKING. It is a binary choice exercise that is useful in <u>sorting out preferences on deal structure, timing, and value</u>. The exercise is accomplished by first defining six to eight ownership transfer scenarios. *(There is no required number.*

You want to look at the scenarios that __might__ happen or that you __might__ consider.) Once these scenarios are established as viable alternatives, the next step is to consider them two by two. And then choose your preference between just those two specific scenarios. By working through the matrix in this manner, the sequential choices will eventually surface your preferences.

Here is an example. This process is best demonstrated by working through an example that could be typical for a business owner. Here is the process examined in a step by step manner.

Step one: Establish an array of potential transfer options. These might be as shown in Scenarios A through F below: *(Your case may be different.)*

Scenario A: Maintain ownership over the long term by hiring professional management and a CEO to relieve you of all direct operating responsibility.

Scenario B: Sell the business at price of "X" within one year. (Where "X" equals the invested capital estimate of value for the business. Net cash will be the result of tax impacts and payment of existing debt owed by the business. This picture of the transaction and the outcome for the owner should come directly from the business valuation summary graphic.)

<u>Scenario C</u>: Sell the business in 3 to 5 years at a price of 1.5 times "X." (The resulting cash to the seller would be projected by preparing a similar summary graphic to estimate the tax impact and the amount of debt to be liquidated.)

<u>Scenario D</u>: Sell the business in 7 to 10 years at a price of two (2.0) times "X." (Develop the required graphic summary to provide the cash to owner picture.) Note: Doubling of value in 10 years would be the result of slightly more than a 7% compound growth rate. Doubling of value in seven years would be slightly greater than a 10% compound growth rate of value.

As in Scenario C, these forecasts in Scenario D must be based on sound planning and a high degree of confidence that the projected outcomes can be achieved.

<u>Scenario E</u>: Complete a 60% recapitalization in the next year at a price of "X." In this scenario, the retained 40% ownership would be transferred at a price equal to (or greater than) two "X" within a seven-year period. In this scenario, the <u>current owner would remain in place</u> to provide the leadership for the business under the guidance of the new control owner.

<u>Scenario F</u>: This scenario would be the same as Scenario E except the <u>seller would be part of the management</u>

team for less than two years. This scenario requires a strong management group to be in place to execute growth plans.

Once the array of possible scenarios is clearly established and understood, the second step in this exercise can be taken. *(There is no magic number of scenarios. You want to include any outcome you could or would consider...but only those.)*

Step two: In this step, for the example, Scenarios A through F are compared on a binary basis. To start, Scenario A would be compared first to Scenario B. Your preference between just these two scenarios would be recorded as a result in this sub step within step two. This process would be continued by comparing A to C, A to D, A to E, and A to F. These results should be recorded for this first sub step and decision. The same procedure should be applied to the binary groupings for B through F.

Let's take a look at how the preferences might be for the binary comparisons for Scenario A. In this example, let's say your preference between A and B is A. Your preference between A and C is C. Your preference between A and D is D. Your preference between A and E is E and your preference between A and F is F. These results would be recorded for tabulation before moving on to the next comparative group of binary options. (In this part of the process, each scenario except B received one vote based on the preferences stated in the review. These are the votes that will be tabulated to help clarify your overall preferences.)

After working through all of these binary choices the resulting matrix might look like this chart of preferences.

Compare A to Others		Preference		Compare B to Others		Preference
A	B	A		B	A	A
A	C	C		B	C	C
A	D	D		B	D	D
A	E	E		B	E	E
A	F	F		B	F	F

Compare C to Others		Preference		Compare D to Others		Preference
C	A	C		D	A	D
C	B	C		D	B	D
C	D	C		D	C	C
C	E	C		D	E	D
C	F	C		D	F	F

Compare E to Others		Preference		Compare F to Others		Preference
E	A	E		F	A	F
E	B	E		F	B	F
E	C	C		F	C	C
E	D	D		F	D	F
E	F	F		F	E	F

The summary "tally" from the binary matrix testing yields a first look at the preference in this example. <u>This example shows that there is sufficient energy</u>

to manage the business through a value-engineering phase to close a perceived valuation gap. It also shows that a recapitalization is of interest with certain constraints. A further look at this second option might cause a modification in Scenario F to prepare for a recapitalization in two to three years in conjunction with the readiness effort inherent in Scenario C. This movement in timing for Scenario F would clearly fit with C for planning purposes.

Scenario	Tally	Preliminary Assessment:
A	2	Little interest in holding with professional management
B	0	No interest is immediate sale at Price "X"
C	10	Clear preference for sale in 3 to 5 years at increased value
D	6	Enough interest in the longer planning horizon to be an option
E	4	Less interest in recapitalization with long-term commitment
F	8	Strong interest in recapitalization with earlier exit/potential upside

Ray Miles, master business valuator and founder of the Institute of Business Appraisers, taught me to use this binary thinking technique to help clients. It works. He presents an application of this approach in his book "How to Price a Business".

The power of the exercise comes from reflection on the why! In other words, think about why a specific scenario was the highlight. In this example, thinking more about what appeals to you in Scenario F and the way it is constructed might provide a targeted path. To extend the exercise, you might modify Scenario F slightly and then compare it again to Scenario C.

This technique should help you in your personal preparation for a transaction by defining and ranking a variety of objectives. The specific timeframes can be instrumental in gaining momentum for any personal changes required to increase "readiness." You should be more ready after the first iteration of this "thinking exercise," and you should notice improvements as you further iterate the process to reference your preferences.

It should be remembered that the scenario statements are for the value of the invested capital. Given that the tax impact as well the remaining debt in the capital structure will change over time, the net seller's cash flow may be greater than the simple invested capital multiple referenced; i.e. the increase in net cash for Scenario C might be twice or more than that of Scenario B. Similarly, the net cash to the seller in Scenario F (as modified) will arrive in two lumps and might be in the same range after allowing for the time value of money.

These cash projections are just that…projections. They do show how business performance improvement will increase value over time with solid plans and expert management efforts. They do not directly show the risk of actually achieving the objectives; that is, the qualitative measurement that you are applying in the binary preference decisions. Business operations have risks. Small or mid-sized businesses have greater risks then multi-nationals. The "bird-in-the-hand" component is inherently part of the business and personal preparation and the corresponding decisions made.

You can expand the benefits from this systematic preference exercise by also testing downside scenarios. This approach would include scenarios that have less future benefit at some probability level as well as the stated target results; i.e. a scenario option with a 50% probability of no value increase and a 50% probability of reaching the target value. The extension of this methodology should be helpful to expand the thinking involved and to add comfort with the final preference you develop.

Family Considerations: If your family is directly working in the business, then scenarios related to those potentialities should become part of the binary matrix. Direct consideration of scenarios driven by family considerations should help immeasurably in sorting out what you want and what you think is best for the individual family members. This work is not easy. It is, however, very important in your personal readiness journey. Knowing what you want to see occur and why is the foundation for serious family discussions and the related planning requirements.

The family scenarios might be part of a recapitalization, or they may be the driver for a scenario such as Scenario A. Alternate scenarios might include purchase of another business or funding additional education for a career change for a family member. The better you can define scenarios that are both possible and productive...the better you can sort out your feelings and those of folks surrounding you.

It is important to remember that <u>movement toward optimal readiness for both you and your business is the objective</u>. Keeping that in view at all times will provide the energy and focus to work through and understand:

- where you are going
- how you expect to get there
- who will be part of the process

**"OK, so maybe I should have accepted
that final offer!"**

More than one seller has stepped back from an offer that they should have embraced. This is typically the result of not being personally ready for the transition.

It is exceedingly important to know that:

When you get *there*...
You are *there*!

You want to remember that the objective is to **"sell the business without regrets."** Unfortunately, poor planning and lack of personal preparation can create a mismatch between the readiness of the business, the market, and you...the seller. The sooner you get yourself ready for a transaction, the sooner you will reduce the likelihood that you will miss an important opportunity.

Chapter 7

The Market and "The" Market

The third part of the answer is: <u>When the market is ready</u>! That seems like a simple enough statement as long as we don't ask… which market. Are we talking about: the stock market? the bond market? the real estate market? the commodities market? Or are we talking about all of these markets and "the" market for small to midsize businesses in general. Or are we talking about "the" market for privately-held businesses in a particular industry? Or an industry sector?

So…we have to determine which market, or combination of markets, we need to focus on before we can determine whether "the" market is ready!

The Economy: The backdrop to the various markets is the general economic condition. These conditions are measured by GDP growth both domestically and internationally. The prospects for changes in market conditions are driven by a reflective of various factors. GDP growth measures changes in the economy in general within its larger cycles. This is a starting point for a thorough review. A look at your business through the last one or two larger economic cycles will provide you with this all important connection. A direct correlation may be evident, or it may become apparent that there is little correlation.

Did your business revenue decline in lockstep with any GDP decline? GDP tends to rise or fall in small, single digit percentages as shown in the chart below. Were these smaller movements representative of what happened in your business? Or was the impact much more dramatic? The precise answers to this question is certainly related to which cycle is under review. And which parts of the larger economy contributed to the observed variations.

The more important questions may be which industry or industries most affect your business. Many businesses experience revenue drops at 5 to 10 times the reduction in GDP growth. A decline of 2 or 3% in GDP growth can often mean a revenue decline of 15 to 30% in some industries, and that much or more in specific privately-held businesses.

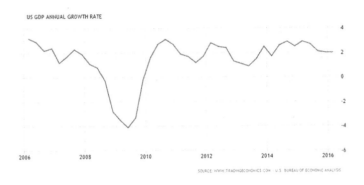

Depending on the operating leverage in your business, a revenue decline of 30% could easily take your business from a highly-profitable position to a position of substantial loss. Clearly, you do not want to place your business on the market during or shortly after such a performance decline, so it's important to be keenly aware of these larger economic cycles and the associated risks.

Consequently, you want to develop the skills to regularly monitor the economy. GDP growth rates and the related trends should be used for general planning purposes. A closer look at unemployment rates will provide additional insight into the stage of a particular economic cycle. Ideally you want to place your business on the market during a stable or an accelerated growth period. The weekly jobless claims are a good indicator of the employment trends. Claims levels above 400,000 indicate recession and levels below 300,000 suggest solid underlying economic activity. The movement in these levels is what you want to monitor.

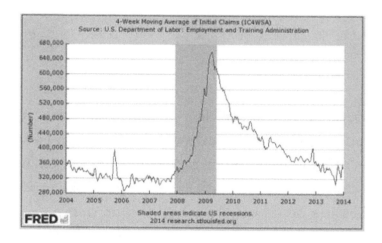

This is the backdrop that you can use to reduce buyers concerns of general economic risks. It also defines the timeframe in which your business is more likely to be exhibiting solid revenue and income growth. Think of this as canoeing downstream and not up! (The graphic history shown for the 10-year period from 2004 through 2014 shows that 7 out of 10 years provided a positive market background...by this measure.)

The other important indicator of future economic activity is the <u>Index of Twelve Leading Indicators</u>. These are available indicators of the cyclical change in the U. S. economy. When the indicators turn down to a level below the year-ago levels, a recession is likely. Conversely, these indicators turn up in advance of an economic recovery. The predictive record of these measures has been excellent since WWII. Each month, the Commerce Department issues the composite index of the twelve indicators. Monitoring this information can provide a solid basis for timing the sale of your business. These indicators are also very useful in capital equipment investment decisions.

General Investment Environment: The relative position and cycles within the public markets are important in a number of aspects. First, when the public markets are advancing, there is a significantly more positive attitude among potential acquirers. This is the same phenomenon that you see when a local professional sports team is winning. It has the ability to cause investors (buyers) to focus more on the rewards of future ownership and less on the risks.

Second, the public markets, both stocks and bonds, are going to be driven by a number of variables. The relative level of interest rates and inflation will be reflected in bond yields and possibly in stock prices. The required rates of return for buyers will be related to these "comparable" investments...based on the principle of alternatives. A good understanding of these markets and their cyclical nature will be helpful in a number of respects.

One related aspect to this public market is the knowledge that acquirers may directly or indirectly position and pull acquisition funds from these markets. A public acquirer may want to use an increasing stock price as acquisition currency. An individual acquirer may convert long-term investments in public markets to cash to secure equity for the transaction. So it is easy to see that the public markets may have more than just a tangential effect on your pool of prospective buyers.

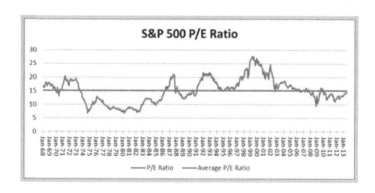

One key variable to monitor is the S&P 500 P/E Ratio. This ratio on trailing earnings has averaged 15:1 over a long period. Movement above or below this level are indications of the relative value of the markets. This ratio can be used to determine where the market is and where it is likely to go over the next few years.

Assessment of these markets doesn't require you to be a professional investment analyst. What it does require is an awareness that is sufficient enough for effective planning. You're not going to be timing the market in particular. <u>What you want is to be in sync with the right trends</u>. If the S&P P/E Ratio for prospective earnings fall below the historic measure, clearly public company earnings are expected to contract. This would signal a notable turn in any upward earning movements, which might influence the pool of buyers.

It is all about understanding any change in the trends!

The Industry: Analysis of the subject business's industry is much the same. Are growth trends in place or vice versa? Is the industry in favor or vice versa? Are changes in the general economy impacting industry prospects? Are prospective buyers going to see an investment in this industry as carrying a normal rate of return and associated risk? Information should be readily available on your primary industry and already integrated into your strategic and business plans.

Understanding the industry and the factors required for success is critical. Key among these most basic of factors are:

- What is the size of the market or key market segment?
- What is the growth rate for the market or market segment?
- What is the market impact of technology or other changes?

A big, big question is: Can your business move beyond the trends in your industry? You want to able to answer: Certainly! Adoption of sound strategic plans and development of exceptional products can have that result. Experienced management teams can normally moderate the impact of any negative industry trend. If this case can be demonstrated, that is excellent. Plus, such characteristics should permit your business to be ready throughout a large portion of the typical cycles.

Analysis could show a much different picture. You may have a business that thrives in down cycles. That understanding and what it means to business performance should drive your evaluation of "the" market for YOUR business. For a business with counter cyclical attributes, market indicators should be assessed in a similar manner but applied in a much different way.

Regular analysis of your competitors and how they operate their businesses is important in the market assessment and planning process. Knowledge of their strengths and weaknesses is important to your overall strategic choices. The relative changes in this area should be noted. This is where opportunities surface...or where problems develop.

Professional acquirers are going to look specifically at the perceived and actual competitive position of the business. They will ask:

- What are the competitor's strengths and weaknesses?
- How do the business's strengths and weaknesses match up?
- Who are the market leaders? Why are they in that position?
- What is the company's market share? Is it growing?
- What is the company's competitive advantage?
- Is the competitive advantage protected? How?

Beyond the planning benefits, it is important to recognize that your competitors may be seen as alternate acquisition candidates. Information on their growth rates, financial positions, new product developments, as well as for their key managers is essential ongoing analysis. These competitive businesses are an integral part of "the" market. The market is made up of similar privately-held businesses.

Related Industries: An analysis of related industries should also be a part of your work in this area. As buyers judge the investment horizon, they may be equally comfortable in a substitute industry. This may be the best option in the buyer's view. This direct application of the valuation principle of substitution should be clearly understood. The position and trends of your industry and related industries should be of continuous interest.

The other major reason for related industry analysis is to look at potential acquirers. Related industries may be an excellent source of strategic buyers for your business. They are much more likely to be considering acquisitions when the economy and their position in their industry are exhibiting positive trends. In practice this analysis should focus beyond the specific group of industries to bubble up potential acquirers.

Understanding what drives any potential acquirer's business, and how your business might ultimately deliver benefits, can have a meaningful impact. The price you receive for your business will depend on using this information in the negotiating process.

Technology: All industries have the potential to be disrupted by product developments or technology change. Knowledge of the current technology employed within the industry should provide the foundation for decision making. The pace of continuous improvements by your business and competitors should be constantly monitored. A sober assessment of the potential for disruption due to technology or other major changes must be part of market timing analysis.

Capital investments (CAP-X), required to maintain a competitive posture, necessitates effective, multistage analysis. The question that follows any preliminary calculations is whether you, in your personal readiness assessment, are prepared to use available cash or to take on an additional debt load. Conversely, you must determine if it is riskier not to act (invest). This is an area where there are clear interactions between the market, market readiness, business growth plans, and your personal readiness.

Buyers: Buyers come in all sizes and types. They all perform analysis and act differently. That happens because they have diverse investment interests and preferences. They are also motivated at different times in their business cycle and by varied business and value drivers.

Ultimately, when you are seeking the customer for the biggest sale of your business career, you must be aware of the diversity and difference of buyer groups. One or more types of buyers may be optimal for your business. All of these potential acquires should be included in your broader look at "the" market.

© Michael H. Marks

"Of course my business is worth what I am asking, it has amazing potential!"

Financial buyers are typically focused on the performance attributes of your business, the industry growth rate, and the impact of the financial markets. Strategic buyers are much more likely to be focused on nonfinancial components of your business. They may be looking for additional products or product lines. They may also have a keen interest in particular processes that you have in place. They could be looking for one or more major customer or supplier relationships that you have. Nurturing these major business attributes will provide the opportunity for such buyers to step forward.

Private equity groups (PEGs) may be viewed primarily as financial buyers. This characteristic may change once they have taken a position within an industry. At that point, PEGs begin seeking add-on acquisitions and exhibit strategic buyer characteristics. These professional acquirers are excellent at assessing a market once they have a platform established. Developing some knowledge of the private equity groups who own businesses in your industry or related industries will notably add to your knowledge of "the" market available for your business. A close look at their acquisition patterns will help you gauge timing as well. They are not likely to do add-on acquisitions until they have stabilized the management in their initial industry investment. Once that's accomplished, they will be more than ready to consider related business purchases.

Keeping close track of any transaction in your industry should, over time, indicate which PEGs have interests in your industry. Industry conferences are good places to pick up this information. Personal research through your professional network should also yield results.

There are a number of digital databases that track Private Equity Group (PEG) business activity. These databases show the current portfolio (what they own) and where they will consider add-ons. A good place to start a review of this nature is: PEI Services or Pitchbook. You can access this and other web services directly. But it is probably better to do these searches through professional intermediaries who have some working knowledge in this area.

Industry buyers have some characteristics of strategic buyers but they are primarily interested in the benefits of consolidation. They're looking for revenue growth by acquisition as a strategic and tactical step. They may be interested in product lines, key managers you have in place, or other important parts of your business. These, however, are likely to be secondary deal drivers and may not contribute to their overall value assessment. Industry buyers may not provide the type of transaction required to maintain the level of employment you now have. This is not a disqualifier, but it is an important consideration.

Individual buyers are much like financial buyers. Depending on the size of the business, they may be primarily driven by the desire to establish a job. Midsize and larger businesses are typically beyond the financial reach of individual buyers unless they are acting as a group. At times, a loose group of individual buyers may present themselves as an equity group. If you engage with this type of potential acquirer, it is important to fully understand the amount of investible capital they have immediately available.

Regardless of what group of buyers are active in your industry, you want to act. When an industry attracts investments, there is a reason. It may be strong growth trends and improving profitability. First, learn why the buyers are buying. Evaluate all the other market measures. Then determine how your business fits the profile and driving motivations. If you have a good match to these characteristics, act! The hot industry today may not be the hot industry tomorrow. *(That is the purpose of getting*

*your business ready and getting you ready for a transaction...
so you can act...when the market is ready.)*

Interest Rates: Alternate investments have different rates of return. Publicly-held equities, publicly-held debt, and commercial real estate each have different return profiles. Prices for commercial real estate are often directly affected by the cost of borrowing. The activity drivers for real estate investments have easily observable fluctuations related to the availability and cost of mortgage debt.

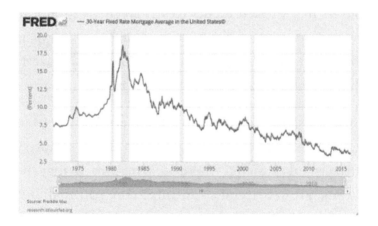

Just as in the real estate business, the relative level of interest rates is important to acquirers of privately-held businesses. The cost of debt will be an expense throughout the period of ownership. Since the prime rate is a base for commercial loans, it is helpful to fully understand the historic movements and implications.

The prime rate hit a peak in December 1980 at 21.5%. Clearly, that level put the brakes on most acquisition activity. The prime rate was less than half the 1980 rate by late 1984 and moved between 8 and 10% for most of the remaining 1980s and 1990s. Borrowing rates found a balance and were not a drag on the solid growth in the economy that was experienced in this 15-year period. Acquisition activity was equally strong in this period of time.

Due to a decline in economic activity (a recession), rates declined to less than 5% by late 2004 and rose to a level below what was "normal" for the 1990s to 7.25% in December 2007. Another dramatic drop in GDP pushed the prime rate to 3.25% just one year later. It remained at this low level until the Federal Reserve began to increase rates in 2015.

Transaction activity levels varied during the first decade in this century. What this shows is that the relative rate in absolute terms is not as important as the trend change and the reason behind the change.

Interest rate levels are a component of the weighted average cost of capital (WACC). As such interest rates will have a modest effect on valuation estimates. Clearly, from this perspective the optimum time to market your business is when the interest rates are relatively low. Low interest rates may reflect low inflation or a recession. A recession can precede interest rate declines. Low rates from this cause are coincident with a low demand for products and services. Therefore, low interest rates by themselves are not sufficient to indicate that "the" market is ready.

Availability of Capital: Professional buyers will advise that availability of debt capital is more important than the cost of capital. Lenders of senior debt capital are very risk adverse. Their appetite for lending can change dramatically based on their assessment of economic conditions. These lenders also react, and sometimes overreact, to specific industry trends. This change in posture constricts the availability of capital. Lenders may go from lending three or four times the cash flow to less than two times. This change will require buyers to provide more equity and will directly affect prices that are paid for small to midsize businesses.

To simplify the reason for this impact, let's look at the change in the cost of capital for a variance from a 70-30 debt equity mix to a 50-50 mix. Given that the equity rate is multiples of the debt rate, this mixed change will increase the cost of capital and correspondingly reduce value estimates...and prices paid. A quick example shows this effect for a debt rate of 8% and an equity rate of 25% and an income tax rate of 40%.

This example shows the calculated impact of the debt/equity mix:

Scenario A: (70% X (1-.4) 8%) + (30% X 25%) = 10.9%

Scenario B: (50% X (1-.4) 8%) + (50% X 25%) = 14.9%

A variance in the discount rate of this magnitude would result in a reduction in value estimate of over 25%. This example is set up to show the impact from limited availability of debt capital. The precise scenario difference might not be found exactly in the market. It is, however, instructive to note that this example is similar to what occurred between 2007 and 2009.

Your business valuator can provide a lot of information on rates and lending patterns. They can help you analyze the rate fluctuations and weigh the implications. Don't hesitate to ask them for this help. Refer to your baseline business valuation report to prompt questions. Get regular inputs and answers so you are following these trends in real time.

Banking has changed in a number ways over the last decade. This ebb and flow of capital availability has not changed. It is occurring today and will continue to be an important part of the market background. You want your business to be ready when the market exhibits movement toward greater first-tier lending. This is where more than fifty percent of the cash you will receive comes from. Consequently, availability of bank lending has a direct effect, as noted, on valuation analysis by buyers.

As professional acquirers move beyond commercial lending sources, their cash flow analysis will change. Inclusion of specialty lenders (mezzanine) in the mix changes the cost of capital and repayment timing. Creative use of these additional capital sources may facilitate transactions and permit them to close under more attractive terms. Use of this more expensive capital will certainly have a potential impact on prices paid. This impact may be more than offset by the improved availability of capital.

Conversely, when private equity groups and strategic buyers have high levels of funds available the competitive nature of the market changes. A look at the amount of cash on the balance sheet of public companies can often indicate their appetite and willingness to deploy those funds. These companies will seek to invest in businesses where they can generate higher rates of return.

The private equity groups are very disciplined business purchasers. PEGs will, at times, stretch to acquire a great business with multiple positive attributes. *(The list of primary business qualities and measures was reviewed in the business readiness section.)* Timing your entry into "the" market can be optimized when the business has previously established elements of fundamental growth and strength.

Employees: The availability of skilled and technically-trained employees has become more and more important to every business. The lack of this basic business resource in some regions can directly affect business performance and certainly can affect a buyer's willingness to complete a purchase. This is another market that must be monitored. The implications can be significant. The cost to attract and retain key employees and effective managers will be part of the ongoing expenses projected by an acquirer. A keen understanding of the local and regional markets for your employees and knowledgeable managers is important. If you are able to easily attract and train sufficient staff to support growth, that fact should be highlighted. A detailed analysis of how you have addressed this market and mitigated any impact on your business can be a major plus.

The current and future cost of healthcare and other employee benefits has a direct impact on financial performance. How buyers include these expenses in projections will depend on what results you have achieved. A superior benefits package may have been used to attract and retain skilled employees. These costs may be a major positive trade-off. How they benefit operations should be addressed in buyers' discussions.

Structural changes to benefit packages that impact employees may be driven by market forces. Rapid increases in healthcare costs and limited choices in healthcare providers have become the norm. Measured reaction to these market forces is important to maintain the balance required. Slightly higher benefit costs with very low turnover in employees is certainly going to be viewed positively by an experienced buyer. Be sure to measure twice and cut once...if and only if necessary.

Tax Environment: Tax rates and tax codes change over time. The business valuation graphical summary showed the impact of taxes on ordinary gains and on capital gains. These rates often change together and sometimes move in opposite directions. A detailed analysis of the impact of taxes on a transaction today and an assessment of what the taxing environment might be in the future is part of market assessment. It's simple...taxes reduce the amount of cash you keep!

If value increases over time but the impact of taxes also increases, the net effect may be less than expected.

Any prospects for changes in tax rates should be factored into timing decisions. The impact of rules and regulations under public discussion as well as the likelihood of rate increases or rate reductions should be understood. This is not where you want to be surprised. It is an area where transactional rewards can be changed or significantly reduced due to delays.

Including the tax environment in the market readiness and timing analysis is important. Although important, taxes are only a part of the picture. It is more important to have a deep understanding of how the various markets addressed in this discussion affect "the" market for your business. <u>You want to understand the impact of taxes but not let them drive decisions beyond a reasonable point.</u>

External Factors: Every business has to contend with a number of external variables. For some businesses, environmental factors may be chief among these concerns. The current legal environment for your industry and related industries should be monitored on a regular basis. Perspective changes in laws and regulations can have a significant impact on your business. Understanding the implications of recent legislation must be factored into market readiness assessments. The compliant cost for new or pending rules are major considerations by buyers. It should be well understood that the associated difficulties will consume precious management time.

The news media tends to focus on negative occurrences or the potential for such developments. Market timing can rarely be used to anticipate major international disruptions in the global economy. It is instructive to recognize that these risks do exist. Consequently, a delay in taking a business to market may ultimately be negatively impacted in this manner. *If the business is ready, you are ready, and many of the various market readiness indicators are in place... it's time to act!*

Chapter 8

Summary

The answer to the question:

When should I sell My Business?

...is straight forward.

The right time to sell is:

When the business is ready!
When you are ready!

and

When "the" market is ready!

The process to put "the answer" to use requires significant effort. There is complexity in preparation and assessment of readiness. This book outlined the major steps and related processes required to prepare a business for sale. Many of these steps are interdependent. The thinking stimulated to develop and adjust the business and personal plans is the source of the created value.

Appendix A offers twenty (20) questions to fire you up to start planning. If you cannot answer YES to these questions, it is a clear indication that there is important work to be done. To move ahead...motivate yourself to complete the following ACTIONS:

- Assess where you and your business are today
- Establish written estate, business and personal financial goals
- Develop written estate, business, and personal financial plans
- Execute these integrated plans to realize these goals

As in any planning process, you cannot begin until you know where you are and where you want to go. A properly prepared business valuation provides this foundation. Engaging a top professional to complete a business valuation for use in planning is the first step. You want to find the right person to do this work and keep them beside you throughout the planning process. Once a solid planning-oriented valuation has been completed, it can be regularly updated. You can then exercise the inputs for use in business as well as personal financial and estate planning.

The formulation of personal financial plans and estate plans will normally identify a "value gap." This is the resource bucket that must be filled with the proceeds from the sale of your business. To fill this gap, you want to increase the value of your business...now that you have a target. This value enhancement phase can be successfully driven by answering the questions presented in Appendices B, C, and D. By answering and re-answering these questions you can get and stay on track. The journey to increase growth and improve business performance should be almost as satisfying as the destination.

Measurement of progress in the value engineering process is important. Good reporting should accelerate your gains by delivering the feedback required to adjust plans and actions. Trend reporting is a key procedural tool. Regularly updating the business valuation will prompt needed actions by helping you to continuously judge readiness in this area.

A major part of preparing the business for sale is to understand what buyers buy. Growth sells. Growth comes from effective planning.

Appendix E reviews the prudent use of acquisitions as a growth driver. The information in this review of top management practices also delivers a solid outline for use in all strategic and business planning. Improvements in value are first going to be derived from increasing free cash flow. You will get these results from effective execution of sound plans.

As part of your preparation, you will learn that professional business acquirers are seeking:

- Superior growth (*Growth > 8%*)
- Consistent strong cash flow (*Cash flow growing > revenue*)
- Diversified customer base (*No customer > 15% of sales*)
- Low CAP-X requirements
- Low operating leverage (*High margins; EBITDA > 15%*)
- A strong management team
- Repeatable systems in all operating areas

Few businesses are perfect. Once buyers see something they want, they are going to weigh the risks of ownership. These risks increase with a lack of diversification in customers, vendors, and key managers. A large part of the strategic planning process should address ways to mitigate these real or perceived risks. These changes strengthen the business as do development of efficient operating systems. As you formulate both strategic and business plans, you want to find ways to reduce risks while consistently increasing cash flow.

Succession planning should be integrated into the overall business plans. Formal work of this nature will help prompt management diversification and your personal preparation for an ownership transition. It will also help surface any family issues that may require a special focus. Your personal readiness will not be improved until you address the difficult portions of your estate and personal financial plans. Family's needs and wants factor directly into these decisions. You do not want to defer engaging the professionals in these areas.

Appendix F provides a list of the advisory team members who you will need along this journey. Each of them has a role to play. These experts have the knowledge and experience needed to help you formulate and integrate all of the plans and to shorten the process. You want to use them effectively. Think of yourself as the sports team owner. You are in charge and need to develop and stay focused on the major objectives. The professionals are the coaches on the field. They will help run the plays to get your team successfully across the goal line.

For many business owners, the hardest part of the process is getting themselves ready for a transaction. The noted use of succession planning is a good starting tool. It realistically addresses your direct business involvement. The emotional readiness is a separate issue. You may need professional help. If you are not making real progress in this area, you may want to engage a business physiologist.

The questions and steps posed in Chapter 5 should be addressed as early as possible. Too many good opportunities have been lost because the owner was not ready to sell. The exercise outlined in Chapter 6 is a good way to force yourself to think about the various scenarios. You may find through that exercise that your preference may be decidedly different than you may have originally thought. <u>Do whatever it takes to get yourself ready</u>. There are recurring benefits to having the business ready…but the larger advantage comes from a timely sale. A sale that may be missed if you are not at least moving on a path to get ready!

"The" market for most privately-held business moves with the economy in general. Understanding the connection and implication is important. Ideally, you want both the business and you to be ready when the market is ready. There are indicators to watch such as added investor interest in your industry. You want to sell, if at all possible, when your industry is in favor, and when interest rates are relatively low and capital availability is high. Monitoring these trends is part of your job. You do not need to be a stock or bond analyst. You just need to be aware of what is happening in all of the related markets and in the key industries. This knowledge will permit you to judge "when the market is ready."

You might struggle for a long time with your personal preparation. The plans for the business may not always yield optimal results. But every step you take to improve the business and prepare yourself will make a huge difference when you get into the high-stakes, deal-making environment. A little extra growth and a positive cash flow trend can go a long way toward offsetting any perceived business risks or weaknesses. And, prepping yourself for the emotional ride toward the closing table will make it a little easier and a lot more profitable when you get there.

The key to success in selling your business at the right time is increased readiness of the three components in the "answer". That readiness comes from ACTION. Hopefully, you have found the tools and the inspiration to do just that...take action. You want to evaluate where you are. Gain the needed knowledge to chart the path forward. Prepare and execute all of the integrated plans outlined. Get ready…be ready… for the biggest, most rewarding transaction in your business life. Act now to sell your business:

- **When the business is ready!**

  (You know now how to get and keep it ready)

- **When you are ready!**

  (You know now how to work toward getting yourself ready)

- **When the market is ready!**

  (You know now how to best use "the" market information)

To stay on track, it helps to continuously remind yourself of the real goal. And if needed, to reflect on the quotes from Jim Rohn, Chuck Noll, and, of course, Yogi.

That is what it takes to sell your business:

- **At the right time!**
- **In the right way!**
- **At the right price!**
- **Without any regrets!**

Effective planning and careful execution can make for many, many happy days!

"Honey, I sold the business and
we did great!"

Do You Want To Sell Your Business For Maximum Money In Minimum Time?

Here's Why Merger Mentor Is The Trusted "Must Have" Resource For Business Owners Around The World ...

Merger Mentor is your one-stop online platform that makes selling your business stress-free, effortless and ensures you sell at the right time, to the right buyer, for the right amount.

Inside you'll get instant access to...

- Proven performance enhancement strategies you can use to increase the value of your business fast.

- Easy-to-use business valuation software so you can find out what your business is worth right now in today's market.

- Checklists, templates and resources for getting your business ready for sale... optimizing how much it's worth and preparing you for the transaction.

And that's just a fraction of what's waiting for you, there's much, much more!

Merger Mentor gives you the most up-to-date, relevant and actionable information to help you sell your business for the maximum amount in minimum time.

To Find Out More About Merger Mentor,
Go To The Link Below
www.MergerMentor.com

Appendices

Appendix A

Planning Initiation Questions

1. Do you have written business plans and goals?
2. Do you have written personal financial plans and goals?
3. Do you have written plans and goals for your family?
4. Have you done an internal assessment of your business?
5. Have you done a business valuation for planning?
6. Have you prepared an estate plan?
7. Have you put a buy-sell agreement in place?
8. Have you put keyman insurance in place?
9. Have you recently updated your will?
10. Have you planned for an ownership change of your business?
11. Are you considering an internal transfer ownership?
12. Are you considering an external transfer of ownership?
13. Are you aware of the advantage and risks of transfer options?

14. Have you established a preliminary ownership transfer date?

15. Have you planned for the tax impact of decisions?

16. Does your financial plan show cash sources and needs?

17. Is there a gap between the cash sources and needs?

18. Will the current post business sale proceeds fill the cash gap?

19. Have you made contingent plans for the "Dismal Ds"?

20. Have you discussed your plans with your spouse and family?

If you answered NO to a question, it shows the need for action!

To get the important YES answers, start by setting a schedule to first complete these critical ACTIONS!

a. Assess where you and your business are today!

b. Establish written estate, business, and financial goals!

c. Establish written estate, business, and financial plans!

d. Execute plans to realize business and personal goals!

Appendix B

Strategic Planning Questions

1. Define business goals and objectives by asking:
   Where should the business go? When? How?

2. Research and analyze target markets by asking:
   Who must be influenced to reach the goals?

3. Research and analyze competitors by asking:
   Who else is trying to influence the target customers?

4. Identify the critical elements for success by asking:
   What specifically must be done to achieve the goals?

5. Prioritize actions and use of resources by asking:
   How much management time is required?
   How should available resources be focused?

6. Initiate immediate strategic actions by asking:
   What are the strategic actions that must be taken?
   What is the schedule for these critical actions?

Appendix C

Business Planning Questions

1. How do you define the business?
2. What is the key function of the business?
3. What is the business's operational environment?
4. Who really provides the competition for the business?
5. What are the conscious and unconscious assumptions made?
6. What are the business's outstanding capabilities?
7. What are the opportunities to improve and succeed?
8. What are the true potentials for the business?
9. What are the goals and objectives for the business?
10. What are the primary policies in place? Is change required?
11. What are the strategies in use? Do they need to be changed?
12. How should key projects be developed? Managed?
13. What are the priorities set for projects?

14. Is the current organizational structure optimal?

15. What key parts of the business require development?

16. What are the resources needed to reach the objectives?

17. What are the budget requirements to reach the objectives?

18. What are the measureable results for the plan?

19. What are the benefits to be derived from the plan?

20. What reporting (feedback system) is needed to monitor. Measure, and re-plan, as required, to reach the objectives?

© Michael H Marks

"Marketing plan? Actually, we've had some pretty strong days around here over the years. We know when we open that door today, we might just have another one!"

Appendix D

Market Knowledge Questions

Market research is a critical function within any organization. To succeed, every business should endeavor to learn "what it needs to know" and figure out how to acquire that information in a timely manner.

<u>Information on markets or market segments should initially answer the following questions</u>:

1. How big is the pie?

   (What is the estimate of the market size in $?)

2. How big is the current slice of the pie held by your company?

   ($ or # of key customers)

3. Who has the biggest slice of the pie?

   (Who is the market segment leader in $ terms?)

4. What is the current market leader doing right?

5. What might this market leader be doing wrong?

6. Who has the second largest slice of the pie?

7. What are the strategies that have been adopted by these top two market segment leaders?

8. How does your company measure up, in terms of $, # of key customers, strategy execution, etc.?

9. What can your company strategically do next to become the leader in the market segment?

10. How long will it take to become the market segment leader as you define leadership?

As information is developed and organized on any market segment, it should become very clear:

1. Who are the *key customers* in the market segment?

2. Who are the actual *end users* of the products provided by these customers?

3. Who are the *decision-makers* in these companies?

4. Who are the *key influencers* in each of these companies?

5. Are there other *critical supporters of decisions* inside these companies? Who are they?

6. What do these end-users, decision-makers, influencers, and critical decision supporters value most?

7. Who is currently providing this value for them? Is this supplier providing the desired level of value (benefits)?

8. How are the key customers and current suppliers assuring the delivery of value? (i.e. what are their strategies and tactics?)

Development of market knowledge is a process that should have the highest priority within any company. Work to complete the picture of *"What is happening"* and *"Why is it happening in a certain way"!*

Appendix E

Using Acquisitions as a Growth Driver

By most measures, the majority of acquisitions do not realize their financial objectives. To improve these results, a clear focus and understanding of the approach required for value creation is a must.

There have been many studies of mergers and acquisitions that unfortunately offer limited insight into:

What to do!
and
Why to do it!

The fuzzy information in most of the analysis and review in this area is the result of poorly stated or hidden strategies in merger and acquisition planning. Far too many transactions have cost reduction as the primary driver...even though the publicly-stated objectives are much different. In addition, "industry roll-ups" and "purchases of depressed assets" rarely yield the promised returns-on-investment.

A better approach is to follow the logic spelled out by Goesdhar, Koller and Wessels in a 2010 article in Corporate Finance Practice. These professionals outline a simple reference list for use in developing and executing acquisition strategies that can and should increase business value. Specifically, the authors argue that to create value...a planned acquisition should be solidly based on one or more of the following strategies:

- Improving performance of the target company (*This objective must be based on existing knowledge and management expertise.*)

- Removing excess capacity from an industry (*In the middle-market, this strategy is only operative in smaller market segments.*)

- Acquiring skills, products, or technology quicker or at lower cost vs. internal development (*These new assets must be applied to a known market.*)

- Creating market access for products (*Finding new channels and customer base for existing products as part of established growth processes.*)

- Identifying early-stage, developing companies that have a competitive edge (*This approach requires a willingness to invest in growth.*)

Each transaction must have its own strategic logic. Successful acquirers have the discipline to insist on a well-defined objective and an easily understood acquisition plan before moving ahead with any potential deal. In many cases these experienced managers have an overall development strategy based on a deep understanding of the risks and rewards presented in the following graphic.

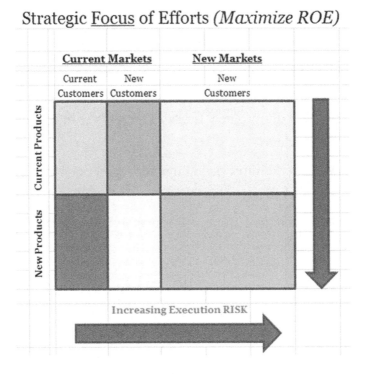

Strategic <u>Focus</u> of Efforts *(Maximize ROE)*

The reason the best of the best acquirers succeed is that they really do not see acquisitions as a growth strategy...but rather as a tactic to achieve planned growth within the business/product/market development matrix. These experienced business managers operate as strategists who have already applied the following recipe for success to their business planning and strategic development:

- Protect existing business with operational excellence
- Penetrate further into existing market segments with current customers
- Extend into existing market segments with existing products
- Extend into new market segments with existing products
- Extend into existing market segments with new products
- Diversify with new products in new market segments

This approach provides these owners with the solid thinking and appropriate measures of momentum needed to execute on well-developed strategic acquisitions to further long-term business goals and objectives. For example: an acquisition could provide a new product group to offer to existing customers as the natural application of one of the five value creating acquisition strategies.

The key is that the impetus would be from planning and assessing that an acquisition (a tactical step) is the best option available. Every business owner should make an effort to replicate this merger & acquisition process to **"increase business growth and value"**.... with <u>minimal risk</u> and the <u>maximum opportunity for achieving sound objectives.</u>

Special Note: This acquisition process review was pro-vided in the Appendix for two reasons. First, to encourage potential inclusion of tactical acquisitions in growth planning. Second, <u>to present the ROE product/market risk matrix for the reader's edification.</u> A deep understanding of the strategic risk variance is critical in all decision-making. All plans should be developed with proper risk assessments to enhance transaction readiness. This matrix can be used as a constant reference in this area.

Appendix F

Expert Advisory Team

- Attorney
- Certified Public Accountant
- Financial Planner
- Investment *(Wealth)* Manager
- Strategic Planner
- Business Appraiser *(Valuator)*
- Value Engineering Consultant
- Investment Banker *(Intermediary)*
- Insurance Agent *(Life, Disability, Casualty, Liability)*
- Business Advisors *(Board of Directors and Others)*
- Spouse

Acknowledgements

In most every book, the author thanks individuals who were most instrumental in helping him or her develop and complete the book. There are a few folks that must be named due to their direct or indirect contributions. This book is no different in that regard.

I would like to thank a young English major who motivated me to learn to write a long time ago and two early mentors who taught me that the best way to address bureaucratic friction is to focus on the underlying truth and facts. I am constantly assisted from hearing these two individuals, Phil Gregory and William Yukanavich, in my ear. They taught me and many others how to get things done in the right way for the right reasons. This book reflects that fundamental action-oriented approach.

My long-time editor, who I couldn't write without, Kim Basile, knows more about written communications than most English professors. Her soft, corrective touch always keeps me on track. Kim has made the difference in getting this book into your hands. I want to thank her for doing the best she could with an engineer turned author to improve readability for your benefit.

My family who has supported me and permitted me to free the time to complete this project. My wonderful wife is a "teacher's teacher." The structure of the book is a direct reflection of the educator approach she brings to every task. I am thankful for her sharing many teaching fundamentals which are employed herein to help facilitate the flow and emphasis required to try to transfer knowledge.

There are many, many other people to thank who have helped me over my varied career. What is presented in this book was learned from the professionals and clients involved in the successful deals completed together. I will always be thankful for the up close view of how consummate professionals and inspired business owners prepare for and close transactions.

Other Resources

MergerMentor.com is "the" educational website designed for business owners interested in professionally preparing and selling their businesses. It provides valuation information, transaction articles, checklists and planning templates for use in the process. This is the place to add knowledge on how to sell your business quickly and quietly at the right time for the right price.

www.MergerMentor.com

Michael Marks is a masterful cartoonist and an expert in database marketing. His years of intermediary experience gives him the insight required to craft the cartoon graphics included in this book. You can access Mike and his extensive direct marketing skills at:

www.ToonsandTips.com or www.Nation-List.com

M & A Source is the leading industry organization for professional development of intermediaries to better serve their clients' needs. The experienced advisors focus on facilitating merger and acquisition transactions in the lower middle market. To find an intermediary in your area or to learn more about this organization please visit:

www.MASource.org

How to Contact
the Author

For further information or to contact the author regarding a speaking engagement please visit www. RichMowrey.com or call Richard Mowrey directly at: **(814) 938-8170.**

Please visit www.PrioritySeminars.com for seminar planning materials. For information on other professional services, please contact your local experienced advisors.

A Request

I wrote this book help business owners prepare for the most important transaction in their business careers. I trust it has done that for you. If so, would you please leave a review on Amazon to help other business owners gain from the important content? http://www.amazon.com/gp/customer-reviews/write-a-review.html?asin=B01LDNKBN8

Made in the USA
Monee, IL
03 December 2021

83792941R00105